LAW, CRIME AND LAW ENFORCEMENT

INTERNATIONAL APPROACHES TO ONLINE COPYRIGHT ENFORCEMENT

Law, Crime and Law Enforcement

Additional books in this series can be found on Nova's website under the Series tab.

Additional e-books in this series can be found on Nova's website under the e-book tab.

LAW, CRIME AND LAW ENFORCEMENT

INTERNATIONAL APPROACHES TO ONLINE COPYRIGHT ENFORCEMENT

PATRICIA WADE
EDITOR

nova publishers
New York

Library of Congress Cataloging-in-Publication Data

ISBN: 978-1-63483-168-0

Published by Nova Science Publishers, Inc. † New York

CONTENTS

PREFACE

The United Kingdom's Intellectual Property Office commissioned two consultants to undertake an international comparison of approaches to online copyright enforcement. The aims and objectives of the research were to establish the range of different approaches currently being adopted around the world to enforce copyright in the online environment; and the strengths and weaknesses of different approaches and to what extent enforcement approaches are perceived to be working to reduce infringement levels. The countries chosen for inclusion in the research were as follows: United Kingdom, United States, Canada, France, the Netherlands, Spain, Italy, Brazil, and South Korea. This book discusses the final report on the international comparison of approaches to online copyright infringement. It also provides the 2014 out-of-cycle review of notorious markets and examines safe harbor for online service providers.

In: International Approaches ...
Editor: Patricia Wade

ISBN: 978-1-63483-168-0

Chapter 1

INTERNATIONAL COMPARISON OF APPROACHES TO ONLINE COPYRIGHT INFRINGEMENT: FINAL REPORT*

BOP Consulting with DotEcon

EXECUTIVE SUMMARY

BOP Consulting with DotEcon ('the consultants') were commissioned to undertake an international comparison of approaches to online copyright enforcement by the UK Intellectual Property Office (IPO) in April 2014. The aims and objectives of the research were to establish:

- the range of different approaches currently being adopted around the world to enforce copyright in the online environment; and
- the strengths and weaknesses of different approaches and to what extent enforcement approaches are perceived to be working to reduce infringement levels.

---

* This is an edited, reformatted and augmented version of an independent report commissioned by the Intellectual Property Office (United Kingdom), published February 2015. It contains public sector information licensed under the Open Government Licence v3.0.

Finally, in order to accomplish these tasks, the brief required the consultants to identify where research is available on the level of online copyright infringement in each country.

The research is based on case studies of nine countries, primarily consisting of a desk review of policy, legislation, research and data in addition to targeted consultation with government and regulatory bodies, legal experts, rights holders' organisations, and organisations representing Internet Service Providers (ISPs). In addition to the country case studies, the views of the European Commission (EC) and the World Intellectual Property Organisation (WIPO) were also sought to better understand how countries are (or are not) liaising and cooperating on the development of joint approaches to online copyright enforcement.

Background and Context

While the brief requires the research to review different approaches to online copyright enforcement in the context of 'what works', it is important to not reduce the question of what determines the level of copyright infringement to a single explanatory variable – namely, the specific measures that a country puts in place to enforce copyright online. In reality, copyright infringement online is a complex phenomenon to which many factors contribute, for instance:

- Enforcement measures taken in other jurisdictions – as content over the internet is distributed and can be accessed across borders, actions that are taken in country *A* can affect country *B*.
- Technological development – the rollout and affordability of fixed line broadband; infrastructure, 3G wireless and wifi networks, and the penetration rate of a range of connected devices will all have some influence in determining the levels of both legal and illegal consumption of copyright protected content online. While some states in East Asia and in the Nordic and Anglophone countries have extensive coverage and take up of fast broadband services, this is still not the case across all of continental Europe nor of course in developing countries. Although access to reliable, fast broadband – whether mobile or fixed line – provides the opportunity for subscribers to stream and download content that infringes copyright, it

is also the pre-requisite for the development of competitive, legal online digital content services; and

- The availability and affordability of legal services - for most of the previous decade, online legal services for music, films, TV, books, games, software etc. were few in number and not widely available across different territories. Also, where they did exist, they paled in comparison with illegal services – not simply in terms of price but also the breadth of titles and content offered, their ease and timeliness of access and the restrictions that they sometimes placed on usage. However, the last five years have finally seen the development and rollout of legal, cheaper, faster and more comprehensive services. Consumers' awareness and satisfaction of these services is also growing (where measured). However, the pattern is still very different from country to country, and services for some content types (film and particularly TV shows) are less well developed than for others (music, software and games). This is important as there is some evidence to suggest that online legal services are contributing to reducing levels of copyright infringement.

The comparative analysis takes an institutional and stakeholder approach to comparing approaches and their costs and benefits. While at the level of implementation, each country's approach is different, there are similarities and differences that can be identified.

Target and Purpose of Measures

Most countries target infringement from both the supply-side (content providers and other companies that facilitate access to material that infringes copyright online) and the demand-side (individual subscribers).

1. Demand-side sanctions that target individual subscribers focus upon:

- Graduated response letters (US, FR, KR, UK) – warning letters of increasing severity sent to subscribers whose accounts have been linked to identified online copyright infringement, with the ultimate sanction of prosecution if infringement from the account being monitored does not cease;

- 'Throttling back' (US) – slowing down the speed of the internet connection to accounts that have been linked to infringement if this behaviour persists;
- Termination of access (KR, US) – some states have created the right to terminate the internet access for a given period for subscribers whose accounts have been linked to persistent infringement; and
- Fines (all countries) and imprisonment (BR, KR) – countries reserve the right to use 'traditional' judicial measures to pursue persistent infringers, though only in Brazil and South Korea is imprisonment an option.

It is important to note that the first three types of sanctions are extra judicial processes that have been developed across the case study countries.

2. Supply-side sanctions that target mainly companies providing or facilitating access to infringing content focus upon:

- Take down and blocking of sites (all but CA and FR); and
- 'Follow the money' approaches (NL, SP, UK) – targeting intermediaries who either knowingly or not knowingly are involved in monetising online content that infringes copyright (e.g. advertisers and financial intermediaries).

Both take down and blocking and follow the money approaches are also extra judicial processes. However, rights holders and police also have recourse to:

- Legal action (all) – companies can be pursued through the courts, to take down and block sites but also to sue for damages and compensation.

Several countries combine the largely punitive sanctions outlined above with a strong emphasis on educative and preventative measures:

- Signposting the legal offer – some countries (IT, KR, NL) provide lists and directories of 'clean sites' to increase consumers' awareness of the legal offer in their countries;
- Subsidies to consume the legal offer (FR) – France has experimented with providing subsidies to consume legal online content, in the form

of the Youth Music Card, a scheme that ran between 2010 and 2012; and

- Graduated response letters (FR, CA, US, UK) – government sponsors usually class this intervention as primarily educative rather than punitive (KR is the exception). In this, these measures have an image problem as critics focus overwhelmingly on the punitive sanctions that are ultimately enshrined in these approaches, not their educative purpose.

Who Does What

Institutional arrangements and procedures for the implementation of online copyright enforcement measures differ greatly. A major structural difference between countries is whether enforcement is undertaken directly by agencies of the state (FR, IT, SP) or by private actors working together (NL, UK, US and previously Canada). What is more common across the countries is the degree of public sector institutional innovation that has occurred across the case study countries. All countries except BR and NL have developed new governmental structures or processes to deal with the problem. This suggests that:

- existing legal powers and institutions were ill-equipped to deal with the scale and speed of the phenomenon of online copyright enforcement, and/or that;
- creating new laws and institutions has a 'signalling' effect to both domestic and international stakeholders that shows that the issue is being taken seriously. Pressure from external government agencies and trade bodies, particularly emanating from the US, has been a key factor in several countries' (SP, KR, IT) motivations for developing measures to combat online copyright infringement.

Legal system and Traditions

The countries studied exhibit a range of different legal traditions and systems. In particular, they encompass Anglophone common law countries (UK, US, CA) as well as several European countries (FR, SP, IT, NL) and Brazil, whose systems are primarily based on civil law. However, despite clear differences in how copyright is defined within the two different legal traditions, it is hard to identify a determining influence that the different legal traditions have in terms of the policies that countries have adopted to enforce copyright online, as countries that share some similarities in terms of their legal system (e.g. FR with NL and IT) have completely different approaches in tackling online copyright infringement.

Costs

The absolute costs of enforcement measures across the countries are hard to establish. Data is piecemeal and mainly related to public sector costs. Information on costs to rights holders and the cost of court time taken up with cases of online copyright infringement is almost never available.

The available data suggests a wide variance in how much the public sector spends on enforcement in different countries, from approximately £0.8m per year in Italy and £2.5m in the UK, to £5.6m in France and £12.7m per year in South Korea. The high cost to South Korea is mainly explained by the fact that it has the most comprehensive set of measures and approaches to tackling online copyright infringement, and in part is due to some institutional overlap and duplication across the three main organisations tasked with implementing online copyright enforcement.[1]

Having caused conflict in some countries, a degree of consensus seems to have emerged across the countries as to who pays for online copyright enforcement:

- Identification of infringement is usually paid for by rights holders themselves, although some countries (IT, KR) do have pro-active, state-led mechanisms for investigating this, and South Korea also has an innovative web portal that allows members of the public to report infringement directly (and incentivises them to do so through coupons and vouchers); and
- Identification of subscribers is paid for by ISPs – although occasionally this is shared with right holders (US) or reimbursed by government (FR).

Effectiveness

Accurately gauging the level of online copyright infringement in a given country is methodologically challenging and highly resource intensive. Given this, it is perhaps not surprising that only one country (KR) has tracked levels of illegal consumption continuously since their current enforcement approach was established.[2] The effectiveness of policy approaches to tackling online copyright infringement is instead generally measured in terms of 'outputs' – that is, the number of actions that are taken according to each specific policy measure.

Demand-Side

Of the graduated response processes that have been implemented long enough to be assessed (i.e. FR and CA), stakeholders view these as being relatively successful. They point to the dramatic fall in numbers of notifications that are issued between different stages of the graduated response. However, this does not take into account whether the infringement has merely been displaced to technological channels that are not being monitored for infringement, or what the impact is on levels of legal consumption. One academic study in France that does look at the impact on legal sales suggests a strongly positive impact of the graduated response measures on the sales of music on iTunes. However, there are a number of methodological limitations with the study which prompt more questions than answers. While a step in the right direction in terms of improving the evidence base, the study shows just how much more research is required in this area to make any more definitive judgements.

Part of the difficulty in trying to assess how effective the different country approaches have been is that many of the approaches have only very recently been enacted, i.e. in the last two or three years. In particular, while extra judicial supply-side measures have been relatively uncontroversial to implement in most countries, measures that target individual subscribers have been much more so. The debate has focused upon civil liberties, freedom of speech, privacy and data protection concerns, as well as the allocation of costs of such schemes across the various actors, and has brought governments into conflict with both ISPs and civil liberties / consumer groups and NGOs.

Supply-Side

By instituting extra judicial processes, all countries (except for BR) have made it much easier, quicker and cheaper for rights holders to act against infringing sites/enablers of infringement. But in terms of effectiveness, targeting suppliers of infringing content is more challenging than targeting subscribers, due (variously) to:

1) Anonymity – sites that host or facilitate access to infringing content online are almost always anonymous, tracking down which corporate entities and individuals to pursue is hard work and frequently unsuccessful;
2) Extra territorial – many sites that are the source of infringing content operate outside of the borders of states that want to reduce infringement and, depending on individual country law, the government and rights holders may or may not be able to take action against internationally-based sites;
3) Displacement to other countries outside jurisdiction – conversely some countries (e.g. NL) have found that closing down sites within national borders merely displaces the problem as the company simply moves their operation to another country; and
4) Fast speed of infringers vs the slow speed of the law and government – the point above is symptomatic of a wider problem regarding the difficulty of lawmakers and enforcers being able to keep pace with very fast moving opponents.

Cooperation versus Coercion?

Two of the longest standing enforcement regimes (CA, NL) are based on voluntary measures and agreements, and they play an important role in others (UK, US). Joint working between ISPs and rights holders removes much of the friction between actors whose incentives are not always aligned.

However, the ‘threat’ of regulatory action has most likely played a role in facilitating voluntary measures and agreements (NL aside). The existence of laws and extra judicial action can also be seen to have given rise to new, market-based solutions in some countries. For instance, in both Italy and the UK, companies and organisations now exist that provide due diligence for advertisers, to ensure that they do not place online adverts with sites that host or facilitate access to infringing content.

The EU is keen to promote further industry-based solutions in the European context and is currently working to facilitate separate Memorandums of Understanding (MOUs) on advertising service providers and payment service providers regarding copyright infringement. This constitutes a major development as the enforcement of copyright online enforcement has been characterised by a lack of shared approaches between countries, whether at the EU level or through WIPO.

INTRODUCTION

BOP Consulting with DotEcon ('the consultants') were commissioned to undertake an international comparison of approaches to online copyright enforcement by the UK Intellectual Property Office (IPO) in April 2014. This is the Final Report of the project. The aims and objectives of the research were to establish:

- the range of different approaches currently being adopted around the world to enforce copyright in the online environment; and
- the strengths and weaknesses of different approaches and to what extent enforcement approaches are perceived to be working to reduce infringement levels.

Finally, in order to accomplish these tasks, the brief required the consultants to identify where research is available on the level of online copyright infringement in each country. The countries chosen by the IPO for inclusion in the research are as follows: United Kingdom (UK); United States (US); Canada (CA); France (FR), the Netherlands (NL); Spain (SP); Italy (IT); Brazil (BR) and South Korea (KR).

Methodology

The research consisted primarily of a desk review of policy, legislation, research and data in addition to targeted consultation in each of the nine countries with government and regulatory bodies, legal experts, rights holders' organisations, and organisations representing Internet Service Providers (ISPs). Given the scope of the work, this involved multi-lingual research across the countries. In addition to the country case studies, the views of the European Commission (EC) and the World Intellectual Property Organisation (WIPO) were also sought to better understand how countries are (or are not) liaising and cooperating on the development of joint approaches to online copyright enforcement.

The empirical work was undertaken following the development of a case study template. This consisted of a framework of headings and questions that needed to be completed in order to develop comparable country cases. Headings covered areas such as:

- Legal and regulatory basis of approach;
- Enforcement process;
- Enforcement measures / sanctions;
- Costs; and
- Implementation, monitoring and effectiveness.

Draft case studies were prepared based on publicly-available secondary sources and then expanded with detail and additional material provided by telephone interviews with consultees. Once the case studies were complete, a comparative analysis looking across all nine countries was undertaken, also incorporating the insights from the consultation with the EC and WIPO. The Draft Report was discussed with the IPO and the findings presented to the IPO's Expert Advisory Group. This Final Report includes additions, revisions and suggestions made by both groups.

Structure of the Report

The next section provides a short discussion of the background and context for the consideration of online copyright enforcement policies. This chapter serves to caution against any attempt to infer direct one-to-one relationships between the policies adopted in a given country to enforce copyright online and the level of copyright infringement that exists in the same country. In particular, the chapter draws attention to both the state of technological development internationally as well as the development of legal, online audio-visual services as factors that also have a bearing on infringement behaviour.

The next section contains the comparative analysis of the nine country case studies. It focuses on the common similarities and differences that can be discerned across the countries, as well as what lessons can be drawn regarding the speed, cost and effectiveness of enforcement. The remaining chapters detail the individual country case studies.

Background and Context

While the brief requires the research to review different approaches to online copyright enforcement in the context of 'what works', it is important to not reduce the question of what determines the level of copyright infringement to a single explanatory variable – namely, the specific measures that a country puts in place to enforce copyright online. In reality, copyright infringement online is a complex phenomenon to which many factors contribute, for instance:

- enforcement measures taken in other jurisdictions;
- technological development; and
- the availability and affordability of legal services.

Taking these in turn, due to the distributed nature of the internet, the online consumption of copyright infringing material does not neatly reside within country borders. Therefore enforcement action taken in territory A may well have consequences for infringing behaviour in territory B, particularly where the US is concerned. A specific example here would be the shutdown of MegaUpload by the US authorities. At the time of its closure, the site was one of the most popular file hosting services on the net and as such, a very large source of copyright infringing material. The cessation of the service will have affected users and infringers around the world, not solely within the US.

Technological Development

The rollout and affordability of fixed line broadband infrastructure, 3G wireless and wifi networks, and the penetration rate of a range of connected devices (e.g. smartphones, tablets, etc.) will all have some influence in determining the levels of both legal and illegal consumption of copyright protected content online. At the most basic level, the penetration of broadband internet access and device ownership sets the limits to both legal and illegal consumption of online content as without these access technologies, neither is possible.

Figure 1 below, shows the most recent comparative statistics for the number of wireless and fixed line broadband internet accounts per head of population across all the OECD countries[3]. As can be seen, for mobile, the penetration has now reached levels that are in excess of 100% of the adult population (including one of the case study countries, South Korea). However, this falls to a minority of the population for some countries, including even developed economies such as Portugal, Belgium and Germany. In general, broadband infrastructures are most advanced in some East Asian countries, the Nordic and Anglophone countries.

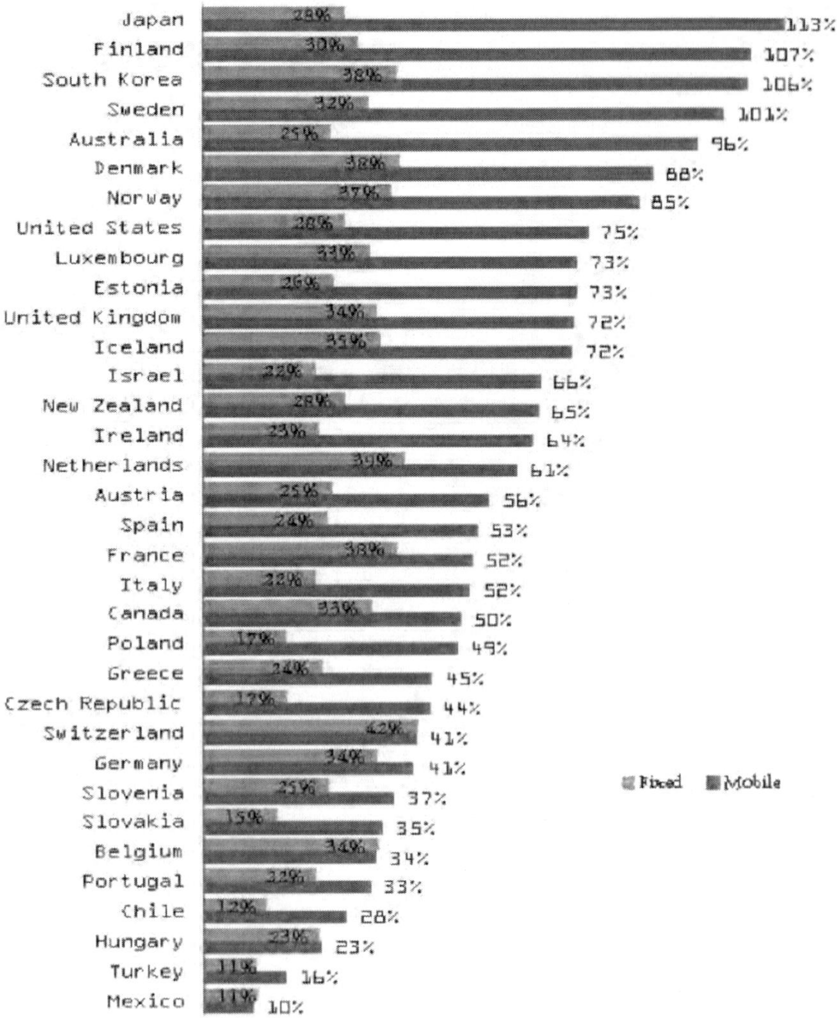

Source: International Telecommunications Union (2013).

Figure 1. Wireless and fixed broadband internet penetration, per adult population, OECD countries, 2012.

This is certainly true when one looks at the adoption of broadband, as in Figure 1 above. When looking at the average speed of fixed broadband, South Korea is far ahead of any other country, representing a long term government planning goal to have the best digital economy infrastructure in the world. While Japan and the Nordic countries do still feature among the countries with the fastest average connection speeds, there are also more continental European countries represented in this group, with the Anglophone countries slipping further down the list. This is particularly notable with regard to Australia and New Zealand, which feature among the countries with the slowest average broadband connection speeds, perhaps reflecting the difficulty of serving relatively geographically dispersed populations.

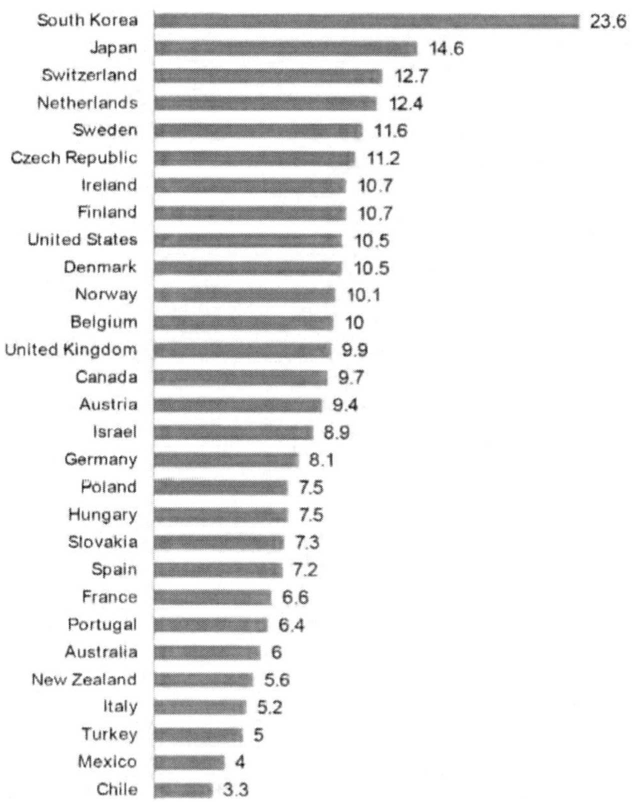

Source: Akami State of the Internet Report (2014).

Figure 2. Average fixed broadband internet connection speeds across the OECD countries, Mega Bits per Seconds (Mbps), 2014.

Access to reliable, fast broadband – whether mobile or fixed line – clearly provides the opportunity for subscribers to stream and download content that infringes copyright. Certainly the South Korean case study below shows that in the mid 2000s, before government enforcement policies came into being, the country was also one of the leaders in terms of copyright infringement (in addition to being a leader in broadband rollout). But when connection speeds are quick enough to support audio-visually rich content and penetration rates become significant, the combination also creates a platform in which legal services can compete. This is not likely to be the case in countries where broadband speeds are slow and penetration levels remain low. Italy has struggled with both of these factors, and the market for legal online services has also been correspondingly slow to develop, relative to many of their European peers. However, the Italian case study below illustrates that there have been additional obstacles that have most likely also contributed to this situation (for instance the level of detail and information that consumers have to disclose to make an online purchase in Italy is more onerous than in most other countries), which cautions against single factor explanations in the development of legal online content services.

Legal Online Audio-Visual Content Services

For most of the previous decade, online legal services for music, films, TV, books, games, software etc. were few in number and not widely available across different territories. Also, where they did exist, they seemed unattractive in comparison with illegal services – not simply in terms of price but also the breadth of titles and content offered, their ease and timeliness of access and the restrictions that they sometimes placed on usage (e.g. through the use of Digital Rights Management software). This is important as, after price, the level of inventory and the timeliness in particular are regularly cited by consumers as reasons for consuming digital cultural content by means that infringe copyright[4].

However, the last five years have finally seen the development and rollout of legal, cheaper, faster and more comprehensive services, such as Spotify and Deezer in music, Netflix, Blinkbox, Hula et al. for film and TV, and Amazon for e-books. As can be seen in Figure 3, in some countries, the choice of legal online music services is now vast, and the pattern is different to that for broadband internet uptake. For music, the countries with the widest choice of music services features many more continental European countries, as well the

English speaking countries. Services are also growing quickly – Spotify, for instance, launched in 38 new countries in 2013 and overall, subscribers to all paid-for online legal music services globally have grown from 8m in 2010 to 28m in 2013. [5]

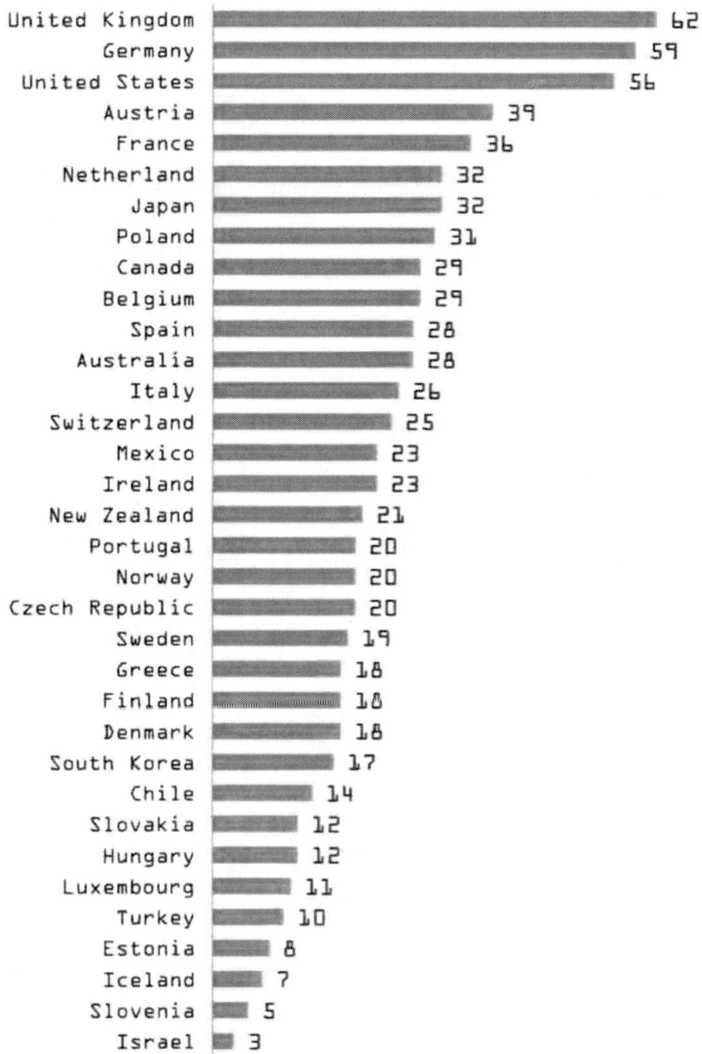

Source: BOP Consulting with DotEcon (2014).

Figure 3. Number of legal online music services available in OECD countries, 2014.

Source: BOP Consulting with DotEcon (2014).

Figure 4. Provision of legal online TV content across the three major, international web-based providers, across the OECD countries, 2014.

As file sizes for individual songs are much smaller than for TV shows, films and most games, it was the recorded music industry that had to face up to the new realities of the connected digital world first. It is therefore no surprise that music has been the content sector that has since developed the most mature market for online legal services. While online film services were the next to develop, online services specialising in TV shows have been slower to develop. For instance, Figure 4 below shows the availability of TV content via the three main international providers of long form, online audio-visual linear content (Google Play, iTunes and Netflix). As the Figure shows, in many territories there is still no legal availability of TV shows via these providers and where it is offered, it is more commonly offered by only one provider than by competing providers. Similar patterns can be found at the national level, such as in France, where consumers' satisfaction with the legal offer is lowest for movies (53%) and TV (59%), and movies and TV are also the cultural goods most likely to be consumed illegally (30% compared with 23% for all cultural goods).[6]

The previous discussion is designed to provide only a snapshot of the international availability of legal, online content services. Clearly, at national level the picture is more detailed, with smaller national players featuring more or less significantly (e.g. in France there are now over 400 legal online content services). The purpose of including the discussion is to demonstrate that in some content sectors in some countries, the legal offer is now healthy and diverse. What is more, where measured, there is some evidence that the awareness of the legal offer is improving (e.g. see the case studies below for the UK and France) and that consumers' satisfaction with the legal is improving (e.g. in France 64% of consumers consider the offer 'satisfactory' as compared with 61% in a previous survey wave[7]).

This is important, as providers of these services are increasingly keen to demonstrate that, by reducing the transaction costs for consumers, online legal alternatives are proving attractive and are contributing to reducing levels of infringement[8]. Their own research also finds support in other existing studies that look at the reasons given by people for why they infringe copyright online. For instance, in the UK almost 1 in 3 people (32%) who have infringed copyright online state that a greater availability of cheaper legal services would encourage them to stop infringing.[9] This view is also held by the World Intellectual Property Organisation (WIPO), whose Director General has said that:

> "there is increasing recognition that a large part of that solution [to online copyright infringement] is the creation of a seamless global digital marketplace. By dint of technology, we already have a seamless global digital marketplace, but it is an illegal one. The task is to establish a legal seamless global digital marketplace. It should be as easy to get content legally as it is to get it illegally."[10]

What these three factors (extra territorial enforcement, the pace and pattern of technological development and the availability of legal services) all point to is the need to remain cautious and realistic in terms of what can be attributed to any change in infringement levels within a given country to the introduction of a specific enforcement measure in that country.

The Online Ecosystem for Copyright Infringement

The review of approaches to the enforcement of copyright online also requires an understanding of the ecosystem in which online infringement takes place. There are a variety of different actors that can be – and are – the subject of enforcement approaches within a given territory:

- Individual subscribers to an internet service provider (ISP): these can either be those that engage in the download of infringing content or its upload and sharing, or both. Infringers may or may not be aware that their behaviour is illegal;[11]
- Online 'content providers' and/or enablers of access to infringing content: websites that host or enable the distribution of content that infringes copyright. The technologies vary and include peer-to-peer systems like BitTorrent and torrent search engines, file hosting (or 'cyber locker') sites (e.g. MegaUpload, Rapidshare) where individuals upload content and can then share links to this content, as well as direct streaming sites. The majority of these providers operate anonymously; and
- Internet Service Providers (ISPs): companies that connect households and businesses to the internet (and thereby the web). While usually not the source of infringing content themselves, they enable 'carriage' for online providers and subscribers, some of whom enable access to content that infringes copyright.

Individual subscribers who infringe copyright rarely do so in order to make money. They may simply be unaware of the fact that the way in which they access digital content online is illegal, or may respond to an – actual or perceived – lack of legal alternatives. This means that the amount of digital content that is legally available online, the ease with which it can be accessed, and the cost of doing so, are also relevant factors in the overall ecosystem.

By contrast, many online content providers that host or otherwise enable the distribution of unlawful content do so for commercial gain, either in the form of individual users taking out a subscription (e.g. file hosting sites) or through advertising revenues. In some cases, these online content providers are connected to 'offline' criminal activities in related fields (e.g. counterfeiting of physical goods and products).

Deriving illegal revenue streams from infringing material is also likely to involve, or require the cooperation of one or more of the following actors:

- Search engines (principally Google): can facilitate access to unlawful content by including sites that host or facilitate access to content that infringes copyright in search results;
- Advertisers: some brands and advertisers pay money to advertise with online providers that enable access to content that infringes copyright. These advertisers are therefore – often inadvertently - helping some online providers to make money out of illegal content; and
- Financial intermediaries: companies such as PayPal and credit card companies process online transactions, some of which relate to various types of payment for content that infringes copyright.

This ecosystem shows how, while right holders of copyrighted work are very likely to be financially disadvantaged by infringement, other actors in the digital value chain are not and conversely, may make money from infringing activities. The ecosystem also shows that policy on the enforcement of copyright online has some links with wider criminal justice policies that aim to combat mass piracy and physical counterfeiting.

Comparative Review of Approaches

Overview

Given the ecosystem in which the infringement of copyright takes place, it is not surprising that there is a range of different approaches to online copyright enforcement. Approaches may differ in terms of the actors on whom they focus (for example, individual subscribers on the demand side or content providers and enablers of copyright infringement on the supply side). They may also differ in terms of the sanctions imposed (ranging from a strong focus on educating users to measures that make it easier for rights holders to enforce their position to applying punitive sanctions to infringers). Measures may be grounded in law or flow from voluntary agreements, and differ in terms of which actors take the lead in policymaking.

These different approaches are not mutually exclusive, however, and often a range of complementary policies will be in place, providing a multi-pronged approach to tackling online copyright infringement.

The specific approaches taken in the different countries covered by our case studies vary substantially, but there are also some general principles and points of commonality that emerge from a comparative analysis. We discuss the commonalities and differences in terms of a number of criteria:

1. Impetus Behind Policy Approaches

While many rights holders no doubt feel that taking actions to enforce copyright online should be a matter of principle, as part of the general rule of law and system of private property rights, in the pragmatic world of government it is clear that steps to tackle online copyright infringement may be taken for a number of reasons.

1. Pursuing a domestic economic and industrial agenda. For instance, in many countries with strong domestic copyright industries (e.g. UK, NL, US), tackling online copyright infringement is considered a necessary part of the wider support and promotion given to these economically important sectors. Equally, taking action against online copyright infringement can be an important policy driver in an emerging country such as South Korea, which is looking to grow its domestic copyright industries as the next phase of the country's industrialisation and innovation.

2. Responding to external political and economic agendas. Less obviously, for some countries online copyright enforcement measures are taken, in part, as a response to demands that originate from outside the nation state:

- Complying with multi-lateral international agreements – for example, a part of the US Digital Millennium Copyright Act (DMCA) is linked to the need to transpose two World Intellectual Property Organisation (WIPO) treaties into US national law by providing greater rights within the US for copyrighted work that originates internationally; and
- Responding to international inspection/ranking regimes – more regularly, a number of the countries studied (SP, KR, IT) have worked to improve their online copyright enforcement measures as a direct

result of being 'named and shamed' by international bodies, particularly those residing within the US (e.g. the U.S. Trade Representative (USTR)'s 'Watch List').

3. Part of wider legislative programmes to deal with the internet. Measures against online copyright infringement can be developed as dedicated, standalone legislative and policy programmes but in almost half the countries reviewed, they feature as one part of a set of wider legislation/measures that updates, overhauls or responds to a range of copyright and internetdriven issues. For example:

- regulating inbound trade in copyright (US);
- regulating the terms of trade between online content aggregators and suppliers, and the legalisation of private copying (SP);
- privacy and net neutrality (BR, NL); and
- other cyber crimes: child pornography, cyber stalking, defamation, and identity theft (NL, BR).
- The other elements that are included alongside measures to tackle online copyright infringement very much reflect the individual political culture and concerns of each state.

4. Finally, dedicated legislation and other policy measures against online copyright infringement also has a 'further purpose, namely 'signalling': demonstrating to domestic rights holders and other governments and multi-lateral agencies that the issue is being taken seriously.

2. Measures and Their Purposes

The case studies suggest that there is now a relatively well established set of measures that countries adopt in order to tackle online copyright infringement. These can be grouped according to the intended target of the measures:

1. Measures targeting individual subscribers include graduated response letters (US, FR, KR, UK), technical measures such as throttling back (US), termination of access (KR, US) and legal action such as fines (all) and imprisonment (BR, KR). Other, less used measures provide incentives to get them to consume legal content online (instead of providing deterrents to subscribers' infringing behaviour). Most typically this occurs through information provision and signposting of the legal offer (FR, IT, UK, CA), but

there have also been financial subsidies to encourage use of the legal offer. Between 2010-2012, France experimented with a 'Youth Music Card' where the government would match the amount spent by young people to buy online music legally.

2. Measures targeting content providers/enablers of content that infringes copyright including legal action (all), takedown and blocking (all bar FR and CA) and 'Follow the money' approaches that attempt to make it difficult for sites that host infringing content to monetise this by getting advertisers and financial intermediaries that deal with these sites to cease their transactions (NL, SP, UK)

In turn, these different types of measures have two broad purposes:

- Educative/preventative: many actions aimed at individual consumers and subscribers have a primarily educative and preventative purpose. Most obviously, governments and other actors are promoting legal online offers better by signposting to sites that are 'clean' and legal (KR, IT). Additionally, the 'graduated response' systems developed by several countries (FR, UK, CA, US) are aimed at education and prevention before punishment (although they can also help to build the case for rights holders to take action against individuals that persist with infringing activity). The South Korean graduated response process seems qualitatively different as it is much more likely to end up in judicial court actions and therefore seems to be aimed more at paving the way for punitive sanctions rather than education and prevention; and
- Mitigating and punitive: other actions are designed more clearly to mitigate the effects of, and stop infringement. For example, the 'notice and takedown' procedures that order the takedown of infringing material, the blocking of sites and the deletion of illegal copies, as well as 'follow the money' approaches that target advertising and financial intermediaries are all aimed at reducing the supply of such material. Similarly, for subscribers that persist in infringement after receiving graduated response warning letters, punitive sanctions may apply, from technical measures such as degrading connection (US) to cutting off internet access altogether (KR). There is also the ultimate threat of judicial action, resulting in fines and occasionally prison sentences, particularly in Brazil and South Korea.

3. Technological Focus of Enforcement

Most territories are technologically agnostic, looking to deter the infringement of copyright by any online method. However, notification schemes aimed at individual subscribers seem to focus on P2P activity, with France the prime example but also the UK and the US. This is presumably because of the relative ease of detecting infringing activity within P2P networks.

The South Korean approach initially targeted one specific technology (the 'Webhard' system) which was dominant in South Korea at the time that legislative powers were granted to pursue online copyright infringement. However, after tackling this through bringing in a Webhard Registration System, the South Korean authorities found that infringing behaviour had migrated to other forms of technology, P2P systems in particular.

4. Implementation and Institutional Aspects

There is a quite a mix in terms of the degree to which enforcement is undertaken directly by agencies of the state or by private actors working together through voluntary arrangements. Figure 5 below provides a heuristic that plots these differences against a second axis that illustrates where the focus of enforcement lies in terms of the demand-side (targeting individual subscribers) or the supply-side (content providers and enablers of infringing content).

The 'outliers' in Figure 5 are those countries that choose to focus on either the demand-side or the supply-side but not both (which is the case in the majority of countries). The Netherlands is distinct for having a wholly private system of voluntary regulation focused on a 'notice and take down' approach only. The French system is the mirror image of the Dutch: targeting individual subscribers through a wholly government-created process and a dedicated institution (HADOPI).

There is variation within those countries that tackle both supply and demand in the degree to which the system contains any voluntary components. The UK has almost arrived at a voluntary system by default (i.e. by dint of the delays to the implementation of the legislation, the Digital Economy Act), while the Copyright Alert System in the US (which targets individual infringers) has been designed from the outset as a voluntary scheme, much like the one that operated in Canada for over ten years before it was formalised in legislation in 2012. Finally, while the approach in Brazil can target either individuals or content providers/enablers and has no voluntary element, it is less 'government-led' than in Italy or South Korea as there are no specific public institutions dedicated to enforcement; it is instead left to rights holders to pursue all kinds of infringers through the usual judicial system.

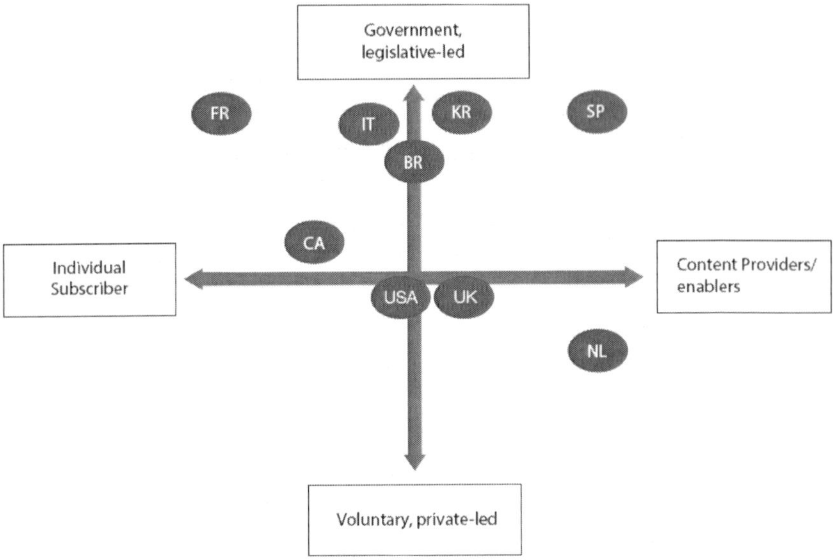

Source: BOP Consulting with DotEcon (2014).

Figure 5. Overview of different approaches to online copyright enforcement across the case study countries.

What cannot be plotted on Figure 5 is that, additionally, three of the countries (NL, SP, UK) explicitly tackle the wider ecosystem (advertisers, search engines and financial intermediaries) as part of their enforcement efforts. As implied above, this kind of approach is typically summed up as a 'follow the money' approach.

Equally, there is great variation in terms of which official bodies or organs of the state take the lead in relation to the enforcement of copyright online:

- Telecoms ministry/regulator: IT, CA;
- Justice ministry: NL;
- Cross-ministerial special vehicle: SP (the IPC);
- Quasi-state regulatory body: FR (HADOPI);
- Split powers between Culture Ministry and quasi-state bodies: KR (MCST, KCC, and KCPC); and
- Police enforcement unit: CA (RCMP), IT (GdF)

In terms of the rights holders, the main difference across the countries is whether individual rights holders represent their own interests directly and individually, or whether a chosen Collective Management Organisation (CMO) becomes a 'clearing house' for requests and complaints and acts on behalf of their members (FR, KR, NL, IT).

In short, the challenge of tackling online copyright infringement has led to a great deal of institutional innovation, usually led by central government. The main exceptions to this are:

- Brazil, which has tried an approach that treats copyright infringement no differently from other crimes of property theft and therefore keeps the process within the established judicial system; and
- The Netherlands, which has avoided government intervention while encouraging non-state actors to voluntarily cooperate.

Across the case studies it is clear that the most important institutions are the ISPs. As the conduits for access to the internet they can see both 'sides' involved in infringing activities, i.e. content providers/enablers and individual users. In order to cooperate with the fight against infringement, some countries ensure that ISPs can remain free of legal action if they cooperate with enforcements processes (e.g. US), while other countries have fines in place to compel ISPs to cooperate and to do so quickly (e.g. IT, KR).

5. Legal Systems

The countries studied exhibit a range of different legal traditions and systems. In particular, it encompasses Anglophone common law countries (UK, US, CA) as well as several European countries (FR, SP, IT, NL) and Brazil, whose systems are primarily based on civil law. There are clear differences in how copyright is defined within the two traditions, with civil law systems being more forceful in protecting the moral rights of authors and placing a stronger link between the rights and the person of the creator, at least initially.

However, from our study it is hard to identify a determining influence of the two different legal traditions in terms of the policies that countries have adopted to enforce copyright online. For instance, taking France and the Netherlands as a comparison, the Dutch legal system was originally based on French law and yet, as noted above, the two countries are polar opposites in terms of their approach to online copyright enforcement. One may say that this might be due to the fact that Dutch law has become more influenced by

German law as it has been revised, and so the comparison is less close than it first appears. But even if one were to take France and Italy, which have more commonalities in terms of their legal traditions, the two country approaches to online copyright enforcement are equally different.

Interestingly, there is a published econometric study – de Dios Montoro Pons and Cuadrado Garcia (2008)[12] – that has sought to look at the problem of copyright infringement through the lens of the legal system that prevails within each of the OECD countries. The study results show that copyright infringement is significantly higher in countries with a civil law tradition as opposed to a common law tradition, even after controlling for factors such as income. However, the applicability of the results to the current study are questionable. Most importantly, regardless of the validity of the results, the present study looks specifically at approaches to online copyright enforcement, not infringement levels per se, and – as explained above – the nature of the legal system seems very weak in terms of determining what type of approach is taken by a country. Secondly, the time period examined in the study is now rather dated (covering 1998-2005) and the research looks only at physical piracy in the form of music CDs rather than online infringement, which has some differing characteristics. Finally, there are also some finer methodological details that may affect the validity of the results.[13]

6. Pro-Active or Reactive?

Most regimes depend on rights holders to identify and report incidents of infringement. The exceptions to this include South Korea and Italy, each of which also have dedicated mechanisms of the state/police investigating online copyright infringement. In Italy and South Korea, the involvement of specialist police units in the proactive identification process targets large scale infringement that is being undertaken for commercial gain. While the UK has a similar unit (the Police Intellectual Property Crime Unit - PIPCU), its operation remains largely reactive as PIPCU still requires rights holders to notify it of infringing websites and to provide evidence of infringement before it takes any action.

7. Absolute Cost

Data on the cost of the full range of processes that are required to identify infringement and administer the respective measures to combat it, as well as monitoring the system of actions and assessing their effectiveness, is not available for most countries. What data exists is piecemeal and overwhelmingly relates to the cost borne by actors in the public sector, in terms of the budgets for government departments and quasi-state agencies that exist to tackle online copyright infringement. Information on costs to rights holders and the cost of court time taken up with cases of online copyright infringement is almost never available.

The available data suggests a wide variance in how much is spent on enforcement in different countries:

- IT: the budget for the telecoms regulator Agcom to oversee their enforcement activities is estimated at just €535K for 3 years, with additional estimated expenditure of the Economic Police Body (GdF) of €810K per annum.;
- FR: HADOPI costs: most recent budgets estimate running costs of €7m per year for 2013-14. Unusually, an estimate has been made of the cost of France's graduated response for both rights holders and ISPs and this was placed at €5.4m and €2.6m in 2011 (ISPs will be reimbursed by the state);
- UK: The government has provided funding to support various measures. £2.57m for 2 years to fund PIPCU, and £3.5m over three years to fund the educational campaign part of the Creative Content UK scheme (with a further £0.5m to support the educational campaign also coming from industry); and
- KR: the 2013 government budget designated for copyright protection enhancement-related costs was approximately £7.5million). The government also covers the annual operational cost of the KCC (a public-private partnership with rights holders), that totalled £5.2million in the same year.

The figures presented in Figure 6 suggest that costs increase with the degree of institution formation, which is a particular feature of both the South Korean and French approach, having both set-up specialist agencies to deal with the issue (more than one, in the case of South Korea). Further, large educational campaigns and schemes that promote the legal offer also seem to be among the more costly options to enact. For instance, although not included in Figure 6 due to its cessation, the previous Youth Music Card scheme in France had a budget of €14m per year.

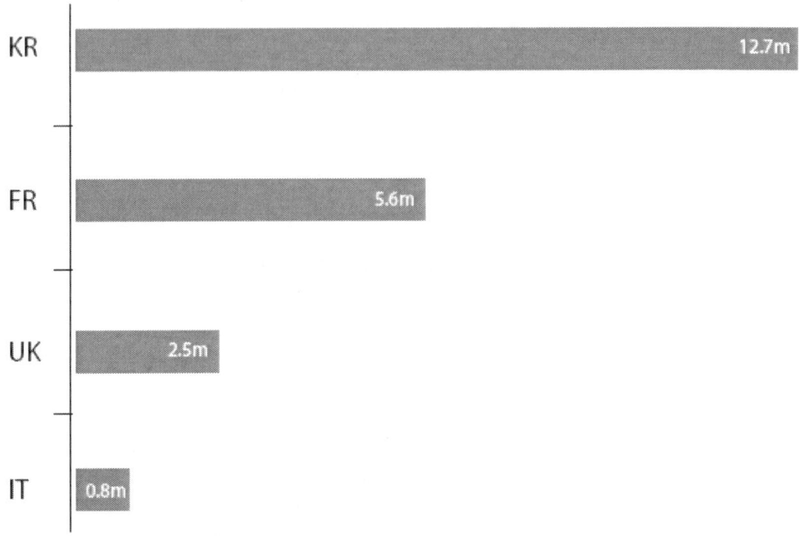

Source: BOP Consulting with DotEcon (2014).

Figure 6. Annual estimated public sector cost of online copyright enforcement (£), selected countries, 2013/14.

Country	Identification of infringement	Identification of subscriber	Notice and takedown
UK	Rights holders	ISPs	ISPs
US	50:50 rights holders & ISPs	50:50 rights holders & ISPs	ISPs
CA	Rights holders	ISPs	N/A
NL	Rights holders	ISPs	ISPs
IT	Agcom (all paid for by ISPs)	Agcom (all paid for by ISPs)	Agcom (all paid for by ISPs)
FR	Rights holders	ISPs (to be re-imbursed by govt)	N/A
SP	Rights holders	ISPs	ISPs
BR	Rights holders	ISPs	ISPs
KR	Rights holders (but re-imbursed by govt)	ISPs	ISPs

Source: BOP Consulting with DotEcon (2014).

Figure 7. Allocation of costs between different actors.

8. Division of Cost

Having caused conflict in some countries, a degree of consensus seems to have emerged across the countries as to who pays for online copyright enforcement. Most typically, rights holders bear the upfront costs of proactively identifying acts of infringement and reporting them, while ISPs bear the costs of investigating notification from the rights holders or government bodies and identifying and notifying the parties responsible for the infringement, as well as taking down or blocking access to infringing content.

9. Effectiveness

Very little to no holistic assessment of effectiveness takes place across the countries. Output measures (the number of letters, takedowns etc.) are frequently monitored and, in lieu of any better measurement, stand in as a proxy for effectiveness. What is typically measured includes:

Subscriber actions:

- number of letters (US, CA, FR);
- level of unlawful file sharing (UK, KR); and
- number of court actions (KR)

Content provider/enabler actions:

- number of notifications, sites disabled or blocked (UK (notice and takedown and court injunctions), NL)

South Korea is the only country to track levels of illegal consumption continuously since the current enforcement approach was established. The UK had a comprehensive monitoring scheme in place in the form of quarterly surveys, but only four reports were issued before the funding, and subsequently the reporting, ceased. However, the four waves of the Kantar Media survey commissioned by Ofcom and funded by the IPO that were undertaken will be used as a baseline against which future trends can be benchmarked. The IPO will be commissioning a further wave of the survey in 2015. In 2013, HADOPI commissioned two waves of a representative survey that tracked both users' infringement levels as well as their use and attitudes towards the legal offer, but this has not been continued through 2014. In other countries, such as The Netherlands, some interesting and quite rigorous one-off studies have been undertaken into the illegal online consumption of cultural products, but nothing that that uses a repeatable methodology on a longitudinal basis. Finally, as discussed below in the Conclusions, a number of the main approaches used across the countries have only just started or not yet even begun (see timeline below) so in these instances, it is not even possible to track outputs.

From the point of view of effectiveness measured by output, the research suggests that targeting the suppliers of infringing content is more difficult than identifying and notifying individual subscribers. For instance, France can point to millions of email notifications and several hundred thousand registered delivered letters sent to individual subscribers. But in the Netherlands, for only 1 in 5 of the sites that are suspected of infringement can the actual infringer be traced. Similarly, Spain was only able to solve 30 disputes in the first year out of the 213 requests that were received in just the first month.

Similarly, although the HADOPI laws have made a notice and takedown process possible, in reality it has only been used twice due to the difficulties of the legal implementation and the scepticism of rights holders that they will be able to ensure 'notice and stay down'. Given such limited usage, we therefore consider that the HADOPI regime can be thought of as being focussed primarily on individuals. In the UK, however, rights holders have been relatively more successful since 2011 at targeting the supply-side through court injunctions which to-date require ISPs to block subscriber access to around 100 infringing websites.

Of the graduated response processes that have been implemented long enough to be assessed (i.e. FR and CA) stakeholders view these as being relatively successful. In both countries they point to the dramatic fall in numbers of notifications that are issued between different stages of the graduated response (i.e. that most infringers desist from further activity after their first, or second warning). Whether this behaviour implies that infringement has ceased or has potentially moved to using different technologies (e.g. accessing cyber-lockers rather than P2P file sharing) or has an impact on levels of legal consumption is not considered by the authorities in charge of implementing the measures. Interestingly, one academic study that looks at the impact of HADOPI suggests a strongly positive impact of the graduated response measures on the sales of music on iTunes (+22%). However, there are a number of methodological limitations with the study which prompt more questions than answers. While a step in the right direction in terms of improving the evidence base, the study shows just how much more research is required in this area to make any more definitive judgements.

Conclusion

In almost all countries, policy has been slow to be implemented, with supply-side actions being the first to be implemented. The following timeline illustrates the main legislative and regulatory milestones implemented across the countries.

Brazil (BR): Lei Azeredo (1999) and Lei Carolina Dickermann (2012)

Canada (CA): voluntary agreement from 2000, CMA (2012), formalised notice and notice regime to come into force in 2015.

France (FR): Act for Copyright and Neighbouring Rights in the Info Society (2006), Hadopi Law (2009) **Italy (IT):** Agcom (Dec 2013)

South Korea (KR): key revisions of the South Korea Copyright Act (2006, 2009), revision of Telecommunications Business Act (2011)

The Netherlands (NL): voluntary Notice and take down Code of Conduct (2008) **Spain (SP):** Ley Sinde (2009) and Ley Lassale (2011)

United Kingdom (UK): DEA (2010) but not implemented yet. First court injunction blocking infringing website under the 97A Copyright Designs and Patents Act in 2011. PIPCU established in 2013 and Creative Content UK established as alternative to DEkA (2015).

US: DMCA (1998), establishing safe harbours for service providers, CCI established the CAS, which includes graduated response notifications (implemented in February 2013)

Figure 8. Timeline of policy implementation per country.

Action across the countries has been slow for a number of reasons, not least of which has been establishing who, within a rapidly developing technological context, is legally liable for infringement activities:

- the individual subscriber who downloads, shares or uploads a file(s);
- the company / organisation that provides software and searching systems to access subscribers' files via P2P systems or that provides file hosting space that individual subscribers can use to upload files that infringe copyright; or
- the ISPs that provide carriage for both individual subscribers and organisations that enable access to infringing material.

It has become common across the territories that ISPs can escape liability provided they take action when made aware of infringing material to which they provide access. This has been established in legislation such as:

- E-Commerce Directive (2002);
- OCILLA in US (1998); and
- CMA (2012) in Canada, which clarified liability and established safe harbour rules

However, aside from ISPs, countries have differed in the degree to which individual subscribers and entities that facilitate or enable infringement are the target of interventions. In particular, until the recent EU ruling, downloading infringing content was not illegal in the Netherlands, which automatically meant that individual subscribers that infringe copyright solely by consuming content (i.e. the vast majority of infringing activity by consumers) have not been targeted. At the other end of the spectrum stands Brazil which, through loose wording of the legislation, has criminalised a large array of online activities.

Countries have been moving to make it much easier for rights holders to act against sites that infringe copyright. Notice and take down approaches have been developed and streamlined in many countries to be very quick (e.g. 2-5 days in the Netherlands; 12 to 35 days in Italy, 15 days in Spain) and inexpensive – in contrast with existing legal options to pursue offenders through the courts. In addition to acting quicker to stop infringing content being circulated, the lower cost and complexity for rights holders means that even small rights holders can engage with the process in some countries (e.g. IT). The UK too has streamlined the blocking of infringing websites since the first court injunction under Section 97A of the Copyright Designs and Patents Act in 2011. However, where countries have set up extra judicial processes outside of, or run separately from the existing legal system in an attempt to speed up the process of acting against sites that infringe copyright, this 'substitution' or bypassing of the judicial system has sometimes drawn criticism (e.g. in SP and FR).

In some cases, stakeholders have also raised concerns that notice and take down regimes merely displace hosting activity to other countries (c.f. the Dutch case). To some extent this is dealt with within the EU, as current law suggests that it is a possibility to obtain take down and blocking orders that operate across the EU. However, this only applies if the infringing sites are hosted within a member state.

While 'notice and take down' activity in most countries is enabled by the existing laws pertaining to copyright, or through previous multi-lateral legislation (e.g. EU E-Commerce Directive), demand-side action requires new legislation to be brought into place. Legislative processes have often not been speedy – Brazilian legislation took 14 years from start to full implementation. While this is the extreme case, the UK experience (more than five years, without being fully effective at the time of writing) also demonstrates the difficulty of getting a controversial legislative proposal through to implementation.

Demand-side actions are more contentious than notice and takedown actions, with proposed legislation and measures bringing rights holders into conflict with both ISPs and civil liberties / consumer groups and NGOs. Conflict focuses upon civil liberties, freedom of speech, privacy and data protection concerns, as well as the allocation of costs of such schemes across the various actors.

The politically charged nature of demand-side actions in several countries has been a major factor that has slowed the implementation of these measures (e.g. UK, BR), and the contentiousness has also left the measures prone to being revoked/substantially revised upon a change of administration (e.g. FR).

'Graduated response' demand-side actions also have an image problem: critics focus overwhelmingly on the punitive sanctions that are ultimately enshrined in these approaches but their government sponsors insist that in the main they are not intended to result in convictions, fines, termination of internet connections or other punitive sanction, but to be a means of education and deterrence instead.[14]

Despite the criticisms and difficulties of establishing new legislation, extra judicial powers, processes and structures, it is notable that only Brazil and the

Netherlands have dismissed the option of setting up new structures or processes to deal with the phenomenon of online copyright infringement. This suggests one or both of the following, that:

- existing legal powers and institutions were ill-equipped to deal with the scale and speed of the phenomenon of online copyright enforcement; and
- creating new laws and institutions has a 'signalling' effect to both domestic and international stakeholders that shows that the issue is being taken seriously (see 'Impetus behind policy approaches' above).

Finally, the presence of dedicated regulation and legislation has, in several countries, prompted both:

- The establishment of voluntary measures as part of the overall set-up (e.g. CAS in US, which helps protect ISPs from law suits or in lieu of a fully worked out implementation (as in the UK, where Creative Content UK has been set up in light of the delays in the implementation of the DEA); and
- The emergence of market-based solutions in some areas: e.g. services to provide due diligence for advertisers (e.g. White Bullet in the UK and the Internet Advertising Bureau in IT)

Two of the earliest enforcement approaches to have been established are either still voluntary (NL) or started out as voluntary actions (CA).

Reflecting on the presence of voluntary and market-based solutions, a general theme that emerges from the case studies is that where good levels of cooperation and joint working between ISPs and rights holders can be established (most obviously through voluntary agreements), this can remove much of the friction that otherwise exists in dealing with online copyright enforcement. Arguably, it also reduces the need for new, dedicated regulatory measures and actions.

This is certainly the view of the European Commission's Anti-Piracy and Counterfeiting Unit, who generally favour industry solutions as the most efficient means of achieving goals. Only if the market cannot find a solution should legislation be considered. Relatedly, the European Observatory on Infringements of Intellectual Property Rights is embarking on a study on voluntary collaboration practices in the online enforcement of IPR, but they are at a very early stage and the terms of reference have not even been published yet. The Commission has also previously facilitated a Memorandum of Understanding (MOU) on the counterfeiting of goods and the enforcement of IP in the internal market, and they are now facilitating separate MOUs on advertising service providers and payment service providers regarding copyright infringement.

This constitutes a major development as, up until this time, what has been striking in the development of national approaches to the enforcement of copyright online enforcement has been the lack of shared approaches between countries. This has certainly been the experience of WIPO, who organised a seminar on the role of internet intermediaries vis-à-vis tackling infringement back in 2005. However, member states were not keen on WIPO subsequently taking a clear, further role in this area and as they only act on member state requests, no further work has been undertaken to develop a harmonised framework or to share best practice by WIPO (beyond the general facilitation of information exchange provided through their Advisory Committee on Enforcement, which has a much wider brief). Finally, as noted above in chapter 3, WIPO takes a similar view to the Commission in thinking that the most effective enforcement mechanism in the medium to long term will be the development of a competitive legal online content market.

CANADA

Overview of the Canadian Approach

The main components of the Canadian approach are a notification regime aimed at alerting internet users to the fact that their account has been used for alleged copyright infringement, and a series of safe harbours that allow internet intermediaries to escape any liability for copyright infringement.

Under the notification regime, rights holders identify online copyright infringement by internet subscribers and send a notice to the relevant intermediary. Intermediaries include not only ISPs acting as a mere conduit but also hosts, information location tools etc.

ISPs are generally required simply to pass on the notification to their subscribers as a way of alerting them to the alleged infringement and a potential encouragement to change their behaviour. Hosts are similarly required to pass on the notification to their subscribers and are under no immediate obligation to remove the infringing content. However, the Canadian Courts can order take down or blocking of access to infringing material,[15] and once a host is aware of any such court decision it must take action otherwise it will lose its liability safe harbour. In this case, information location tools must also remove the material from their cache.

Civil action can be taken against copyright infringers and rights holders can claim statutory damages.

Contextual Factors

According to the 2014 Communication Monitoring report for the Telecommunications Sector, the Canadian Radio-television and Telecommunications Commission found that by 2013, the percentage of subscribers to residential broadband with access to speeds greater than 9 Mbps stood at 56.9%, with 31.4% of all connections giving speeds of 16Mbps and higher.[16] Canada is taking steps to improve further its residential broadband speeds and in July 2014 Industry Canada launched the 'Connecting Canadians' program and has committed to investing up to $305 million "to address gaps in the delivery of high-speed Internet at speeds of at least 5 megabits per second (Mbps) to households in rural and remote areas across the country".[17] Fixed Broadband penetration is reported as 33.28/100 – 5th out of the 9 countries covered in this report for the IPO.[18]

In Canada, consumers have access to the majority of major legal services[19] and there are a growing number of alternative legal services. For example, "pro-music.org" provides a list of legal online music services from around the world that offer music as a download, stream or ringtone. The list is compiled by IFPI[20] based on information supplied by its local industry groups. At the time of writing this report pro-music.org listed 29 legal online music services available in the Canada.[21] For TV and movies, services like the Motion Picture Association Canada's ("MPA") "Where to Watch" service allows consumers to access movies and TV shows on tablets, smartphones and online through a fast-growing number of services quickly and easily, currently providing links to 51 different services.[22]

A recent report by the International Intellectual Property Alliance ("IIPA") notes that the growing availability of online legitimate and licenced sources in Canada is notable and that "Entertainment studios are working with new technologies and a multitude of partners, including retailers, cable providers, social networking sites, gaming consoles and websites, to provide an expanding range of legitimate services that enable Canadian consumers to enjoy movies and TV on a variety of platforms"[23] so there is clearly work ongoing to develop such services. Furthermore, the IIPA report also suggests, "the continued availability of the "free" illicit services hampers the development of the legitimate marketplace and makes it more difficult for it to realize its full potential".[24] However, as part of its "Digital Canada 150" campaign, Industry Canada is promising to ensure that "Canadians will have easy online access to Canadian content" and to provide Canadian creative industries with "...greater capabilities to seize digital opportunities".[25]

Background and Policy Process

In the 2011 Speech from the Throne, the Government of Canada committed itself to reintroduce and seek swift passage of legislation to modernise Canada's copyright law.

This was followed in 2012 with the introduction of the Copyright Modernization Act ("CMA"), which updated Canada's copyright laws to ensure that they are modern, flexible, and in line with current international standards. Furthermore, the CMA amends the Copyright Act by adding provisions aimed at deterring infringement, whilst also clarifying the liability of ISPs, hosts and search engines in providing a service that is used in the infringement of copyright law.[26]

The legislation formalises a voluntary notification scheme for online copyright enforcement that had been in place since 2000 between members of the Canadian Association of Internet Providers (CAIP), the Canadian Cable Telecommunications Association (CCTA), and members of the Canadian Recording Industry Association (CRIA). Under the voluntary agreement, the CRIA notified a member of CAIP or CCTA of an alleged copyright infringement by their respective customers. The ISP then had to notify this customer about the alleged infringement and remind the customer of its obligations under the service agreement with the ISP, which normally includes a commitment not to engage in copyright infringement. The ISP also had to notify the CRIA when it has passed on the notification.[27] If the customer failed to remove infringing material, the complainant could then take action directly through the courts.[28]

The key difference between the voluntary regime and the new scheme set out in the CMA is that the obligations extend to all parties including those that were not involved in the voluntary regime and that intermediaries can face penalties if they fail to carry out their obligations.

The CMA also extended the notion of infringement beyond the previous prohibition of actions such as reproduction or republishing of works (and other actions that copyright owners have the sole right to perform) without the rights holder's consent. Specifically, the CMA added a new subsection to the Copyright Act stating that it is an infringement of copyright *"to provide a service primarily for the purpose of enabling acts of copyright infringement if an actual infringement of copyright occurs by means of the Internet or another digital network as a result of the use of that service"*.[29] This is aimed at actors such as BitTorrent search engines or lists that facilitate illegal peer-to-peer file sharing that, rather than directly infringing copyright in the previous definition, provide services that enable copyright infringement.[30] Any infringement under this subsection is deemed to be for a commercial purpose.[31]

Legal and Regulatory Basis of Approach

The basis for enforcement action is the Copyright Act[32] and its amendment, the Copyright Modernization Act (Bill C-11)[33], which was passed on 29 June 2012 and was published 7 November 2012.[34]

Enforcement Process

Under the provisions for the formal notification regime, the rights holder identifies infringing activity and notifies the relevant internet intermediary.

In the case that the intermediary has subscribers (ISP or host) it is under an obligation to pass on the notice to subscribers, thereby informing subscribers that their behaviour may be infringing copyright. The intermediary is then obliged to inform the rights holder that the notice has been passed on, or if the intermediary was unable to pass on the notice, explain the reason why the notice could not be passed on.

This means that, upon receipt of a notice an **ISP** will have to identify the owner of the account linked to the alleged infringement and pass on the notice to the respective subscriber. A subscriber receiving the notice is under no legal obligation to do anything/take any action. The regime is therefore primarily educational and aimed at informing subscribers that their account is linked with an alleged infringement. The subscriber is however put 'on notice' in relation to the infringement allegations, which may have implications in any future legal proceedings for infringement. The ISP is required to keep records for a period of up to 6 months (or longer if court proceedings in relation to the alleged infringement have begun).

Similarly, unlike in the US, for example, **hosts** are not under an obligation to remove infringing content, but are typically only required to pass on the notice to the respective hosting customer. However, where a host has knowledge of a court decision to the effect that the stored material is infringing copyright, or that the subscriber's use of the material infringes copyright, the hosting safe-harbour no longer applies. Then it becomes a practical matter of whether the host is willing to continue hosting the material and risk potential liability or take down the material.

In the case where the intermediary is an **information location tool** such as a search engine simply allowing customers to use the search functionality to find websites (e.g. Google) the effect of the notice is different. Search engines benefit from a safe harbour provision that limits their liability for certain acts that they engage in as part of providing their services – e.g., caching infringing material found on the Internet – that may in themselves constitute infringement. The safe-harbour ensures that they are not liable for damages, though injunctions (subject to certain safeguards) continue to be available. However, receipt of a notice effectively suspends that protection. Specifically, if the information has been removed by the respective host and the search engine is still caching that material the search engine is expected to remove that material within a 30 day window or otherwise lose the benefit of its safe harbour i.e. limitation of liability.[35]

Enforcement Measures / Sanctions

Notices under the notification regime are purely an information tool. The main aim is to discourage infringement and to encourage subscribers to look into the issue – perhaps there was some illegal activity on their internet connection which they were unaware of.

However, notices may help rights holders in their proceedings in court against individual infringers, though there is no presumption of copyright infringement. Therefore, notices alone may not constitute evidence of infringement, but records will simply provide factual evidence that notices have been sent. How this evidence will be used in court still remains to be seen given that the requirement to keep records is new.

If legal intervention is pursued against an infringer, a range of civil remedies may be sought,[36] including statutory damages. Such statutory damages for general copyright infringement (section 38.1 of the Copyright Act) differentiate between commercial and non-commercial infringement. Statutory damages are set between $500 and $20,000 per work for commercial infringements. By contrast, for *"an individual's potential liability in cases of non-commercial infringement...statutory damages will be reduced to a one-time payment of between $100 and $5,000 for all infringements that took place prior to the lawsuit."*[37]

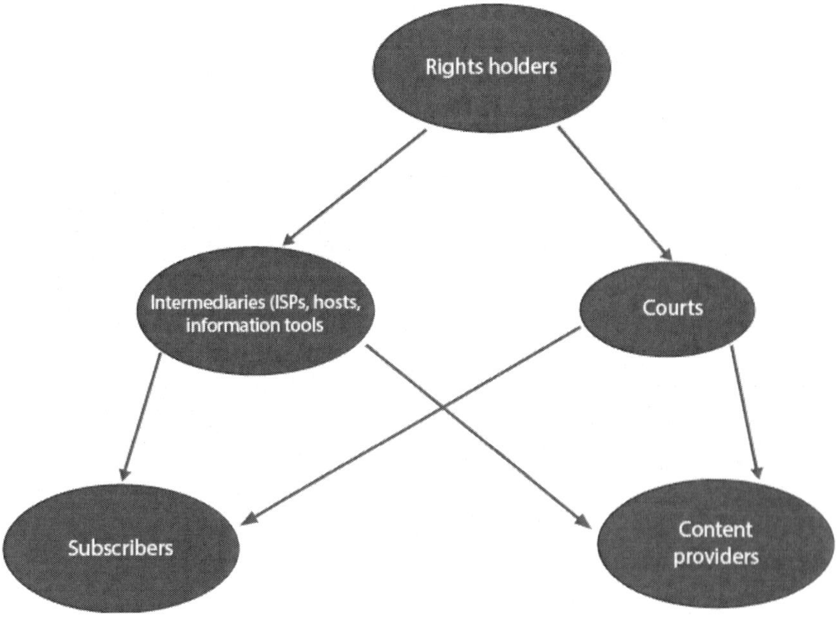

Source: BOP Consulting with DotEcon (2014).

Figure 9. Institutional configuration of the enforcement process in Canada.

The quantum of damages will be determined on a case-by-case basis, generally within prescribed minimum and maximum ranges, including higher ranges for commercial infringements.

ISPs, hosts and search engines are automatically exempt from liability for copyright infringement when they act strictly as intermediaries in communication, caching, and hosting activities (Section 31.1 of the Copyright Act). However, there are statutory damages for the failure to forward a notice without good reason, with damages ranging from $5,000 and $10,000.[38] The CMA does provide the Governor in Council the option to increase or decrease the minimum or maximum amount of statutory damages by regulation.[39]

Burden and Standard of Proof

The Copyright Act does not specify any standard of proof needed for a copyright owner to issue a notice, but lists the information required (including, amongst other things, the work to which the claimed infringement relates, time and date and the location of the claimed infringement).[40]

Any enabling activities of online infringement are presumed to be for commercial reasons. The aim of the new civil liability provisions in relation to online infringement is partly to distinguish between legitimate intermediaries and illegitimate intermediaries – for this reason, acts of enabling online infringement are also expressly carved out of the intermediary safe harbour provisions.

More specifically, the CMA amends Section 27 of the Copyright Act by adding a new subsection 2.4 of which states that in determining whether a person has infringed copyright by providing a service the court may consider:

a) whether the person expressly or implicitly marketed or promoted the service as one that could be used to enable acts of copyright infringement;
b) whether the person had knowledge that the service was used to enable a significant number of acts of copyright infringement;
c) whether the service has significant uses other than to enable acts of copyright infringement;
d) the person's ability, as part of providing the service, to limit acts of copyright infringement, and any action taken by the person to do so;
e) any benefits the person received as a result of enabling the acts of copyright infringement; and
f) the economic viability of the provision of the service if it were not used to enable acts of copyright infringement."[41]

Costs

We are not aware of any estimate of the costs associated with the formal notification scheme created through the CMA. There are some cost estimates available from the previous voluntary scheme. In 2005 Industry Canada commissioned a survey of Canadian Internet Service Providers to assess the economic cost of the voluntary 'notice and notice' regime.[42] The eight largest ISPs (having more than 100,000 subscribers) and around 10% of the smaller ISPs (together serving more than 80% of Canadian subscribers) were surveyed, and their practices and costs documented. The survey estimated the average cost of processing a notice at $11.73 for large ISPs and $32.73 for small ISPs. As large ISPs receive significantly more notices per month than small ISPs (4,426 vs 18), they have established a more efficient process, which might explain the cost difference.

Although the cost estimates established in 2005 are likely to be out of date by now, costs under the mandatory scheme are likely to be of a similar order of magnitude given the similarity of the two schemes. Estimates of the cost of the scheme as a whole (i.e. including the cost to rights holders) are not available.

Regarding the distribution of costs, there is in principle a provision for intermediaries to charge rights holders for the costs they incur in passing on notices provided that the regulator (Industry Canada) has set a maximum charge that can be levied by the intermediary. As Industry Canada has decided not to set such a maximum charge, at present intermediaries cannot ask to be reimbursed. The lack of reliable cost data may be one reason why Industry Canada has refrained from setting a maximum charge so far. This may be something the regulator will address once the scheme is operational and the costs of implementation are clearer.

Implementation, Monitoring and Effectiveness

The formal notification regime is expected to come into force in 2015.

At present, there is no obligation placed on ISPs to collect data on the number of notifications sent, but they may collect the data for their own purposes.

There is some anecdotal evidence that the notices issued under the voluntary scheme have had some effect on behaviour. Rogers (one of Canada's largest ISPs) provided evidence of the effectiveness of the voluntary notice and notice scheme before Parliament – only 5% of its subscribers received a notice of infringement; only a third of those subscribers received a second notice, and only a third of those received a third notice.[43]

The CMA requires the Copyright Act to be reviewed by Parliament every five years in order to ensure it is up to date. 2017 will be the next review and the effectiveness of the notification schemes will likely be raised at that point.

However, there is not any formal monitoring plan of the impact of the regime in place as part of the legislation at this point in time.

BRAZIL

Overview of the Brazilian Approach

The Brazilian approach, contrary to most of the other countries analysed, does not include any special dedicated organisation or body for the solution of disputes in copyright infringement. The strategy adopted in Brazil is instead to have a specific set of laws strongly focused on several "internet-related" crimes, in addition to traditional copyright laws. The complaints and judgments then run through the normal judicial system. The system relies on imprisonment for some relatively mild crimes, to act as a deterrent.

The current framework therefore differs quite significantly from an international trend of understanding online copyright infringements as an activity that requires a different legal and institutional framework to tackle it, often separated or independent from the judicial system. In part, this may stem from the fact that the current law originally dates from 1999, when it would not have been possible to have been influenced by more recent approaches in other countries, such as the HADOPI law in France.

Contextual Factors

Although Brazil is not a leading country in terms of broadband penetration it is a major telecommunications market given the country size of the country's population. This makes the market structure very competitive with the presence of several international players (like Telefonica). Brazil still has a low penetration rate of broadband (45.8%), particularly in the fixed line market (9.2%). This situation has been commonly identified as a limiting factor on the future growth of the country. The 'cold spots' of demand are particularly pronounced in the large rural hinterland outside of Brazil's main cities.

The limited availability of broadband coverage in Brazil is also reflected in a low average speed of connection. Akami's latest 2014 ranking of broadband speeds places Brazil 45th in the world (out of 55), with an average speed of just 2.6 Mbps. However the market is shifting, a new company, Net Servicos e Comunicacoes, started in 2014 rolling out their high speed service (up to 500 Mbp/s download speed) in Brazil's two biggest cities (Rio de Janeiro and Sao Paulo).

Brazil is the only emerging economy in our report. Emerging economies tend to have lower access to legal alternatives, given their reduced purchasing power and limited internet connections. However, Brazil has a large population (200 million) that makes it an economically attractive market. In Brazil, according to Pro-music, there are 23 different legal alternatives for music.[44] The absolute market size has created a situation where Brazilian consumers have a good coverage of legal alternatives. Indeed the three major players in music broadcasting over the internet (Google Play, iTunes and Spotify) are all available in Brazil – this is particularly relevant as Brazil is historically a country associated with a strong musical identity. Also in the film market the three major players (google play, iTunes and Netflix) are also available locally. In fact, when considering the market for TV shows, the presence of Netflix Brazil gives the country greater access to international TV content than many continental European countries, where no such service is available. However, as broadband speeds remain slow, it is difficult to access the legal alternatives outside the main urban areas.

Background and Policy Process

Brazil, like many emerging economies, faces widespread piracy and counterfeit products. For instance, the most recent data produced by APCM (an anti-piracy group for cinema and music) in 2010 contained a request to block over 1.3m websites.[45] Further, according to music industry statistics from ABPD, from 1997 to 2009 sales have fallen from R$1.1 billion to R$360 million, mostly attributed by the industry to a rise in copyright infringement, though the availability of online legal alternatives in Brazil has been limited until recently.

After several projects focusing on cybercrimes developed around the year 2000 by Senator Renan, a new project was brought under the spotlight - the proposal of the then Deputy Luiz Piauhylino, which later became “Lei Azeredo”. This was originally discussed in 1999. Opinions and first reactions from professionals and politicians were mostly positive. The proposed law used precise technical concepts allowing for the creation of a coherent law, containing all of the necessary requirements to become effective, though very limited in its scope. However, later amendments made the law more imprecise and open to criticism.

A slightly amended version of the proposal was presented in 2003 for discussion and eventual vote. That same year, the project began to be the subject of discussion in the media and political polarization emerged between the main two political parties: the opposition PT and the PSDB party (the project proponent). Eventually in 2008, the project gained an emergency status and received a major update and extension; authored by Senator Eduardo Azeredo from PSDB (and thus the law became commonly known as “Lei Azeredo”). However, the project only became effective as a law on the 2nd April 2013. This was a lengthy process started in 1999, voted for the first time in 2008, becoming a law in 2013 as an update from a previous law of 1940 (DL 2.848/1940).

In more recent times, the Brazilian authorities have become aware of the negative tone of the legislation in terms of its punitive nature for users. The political debate has focused on the concern that the law has created hefty punitive measurements against what is understood to be often common behaviour. The Brazilian federal government has therefore subsequently proposed a global framework (“Marco Civil”) that defines users’ rights, such as access to broadband and internet neutrality guarantees in terms of Traffic speed – which are now considered as greater priorities before the setting of punishments for cybercrimes. This additional piece of legislation was also intended to be a landmark in its formulation format: it was presented for public consultation online with the possibility of discussion and review by the public. Some stakeholders speculate that the government will bring in a ‘notice and take down’ procedure in the near future, but others suggest that Brazil is instead creating a regulatory regime which privileges the rights of the individual user first and foremost. Both sides agree that nothing will happen quickly with the general election now imminent.

Legal and Regulatory Basis of Approach

The current framework is based on a key piece of legislation known as "Lei Azeredo" (PL 84/99 and PL 2793/2011). "Lei Azeredo" replaced several pieces of legislation and now covers copyright infringement, phishing activities, child pornography, password hacking and other illicit activities. Other laws have since then have complemented the framework, namely a law known as "Lei Carolina Dieckmann" (12.737/2012) named after a high profile case involving the publication of private photos of Carolina Dieckmann (an actress). "Lei Carolina Dieckmann" covers unauthorized access to computers and networks, credit card/document cloning, and interruption of connections and internet access. The government is currently proposing a wider piece of legislation for the regulation of the internet known as "Marco Civil".

Enforcement Process

As no dedicated regulatory or voluntary process of redress has been established in Brazil, rights holders' only option at present is to pursue alleged infringers through the courts, using "Lei Azeredo". The Brazilian police, acting at the state level not the federal level, has a task force for on-line criminality but this is not dedicated solely to copyright issues and covers instead a broader class of cybercrimes including identity theft etc.

The concern about using the new law to pursue offenders is that its imprecise wording creates four different crimes that can be seen as common activities on the internet - given the open-ended definitions of terms like "code", "malicious", and "damage" that are used in the current law. The most problematic passage of the law, and often mentioned by several campaigners, is article 285-B that reads:

> "Obtaining, transfer or unauthorized provision of data or information: Article 285-B. Get or transfer data or information available on a computer network, communication or information system without authorization or in disagreement with the authorization of the legitimate holder device."

The wording of the article is imprecise and allows for several interpretations, technically even normal web browsing or saving a free picture available in a legitimate website can be a violation of this law as the user does not have official authorization for this act. Given the vagueness of the wording in the legislation, the application of the law therefore comes down to the individual discretion of each judge.

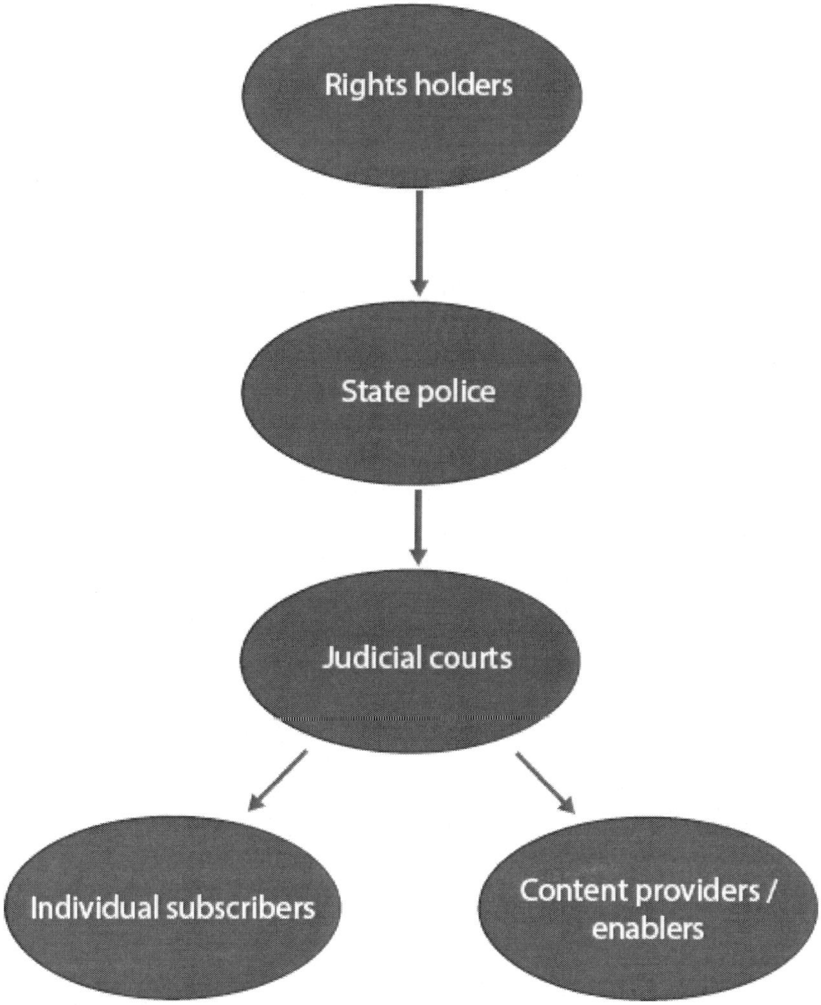

Source: BOP Consulting with DotEcon (2014).

Figure 10. Institutional configuration of the enforcement process in Brazil.

Enforcement Measures / Sanctions

"Lei Azeredo" covers several copyright infringements but it is also a complement to the general law about copyright (184/Código Penal and Lei 9.610/98), which also encompasses the crimes of the illegal copying of movies, music and software. Under the new law, copyright breaches for movies and music can lead to prison sentences of three to nine months in the general case, and from two to four years if the crime is related to a profit-making activity. For software infringement, the general case ranges from six months to two years and from one to four years for profit making activities.

Burden and Standard of Proof

The standard of proof appears to be theoretically very low as the law is very imprecise in its wording. Under the current law almost every mundane activity on the internet can be perceived as a breach of copyright, therefore the real evaluation of the framework really depends on how judges apply the law.

Costs

The cost of identification of infringement lies with rights holders, as does the cost of any legal proceedings taken out against infringers. At this time, the quantum of these costs is not known. The police will also bear some costs in the investigation of alleged infringement but again, these are not tracked and recorded.

Implementation, Monitoring and Effectiveness

The law is relatively recent to come into effect. As there is no special institutional process or vehicle related to the phenomenon of online copyright enforcement, there are equally no plans to systematically monitor the effectiveness of the 'approach'. The most available data shows that for 2010 there were requests to take down 1,329,142 links, 24,637 torrents and 255,626 blog posts. This was only marginally greater (0.44%) compared with 2009.

FRANCE

Overview of the French Approach

The French approach is characterised by an overwhelming focus on the demand-side of copyright infringement, that is, a focus on individual internet subscribers and their consumption behaviours. The key constituent of the French approach has been the establishment of an independent public agency entirely dedicated to online copyright infringement, HADOPI *(Haute Autorité pour la Diffusion des Œuvres et la Protection des Droits sur Internet*; in English: the High Authority for Transmission of Creative Works and Copyright Protection on the Internet), which serves as an intermediary between internet users, right holders, ISPs and the French Penal Courts. Most prominently, HADOPI has instigated a three stage graduated response procedure against individuals suspected of acts of infringement committed on P2P networks. While the end game of the three stage process is a series of punitive sanctions (fines and technical measures to restrict the performance of internet access), the main purpose of the three stage notification process is pedagogical – to educate consumers about copyright. This pedagogical strand of HADOPI's work is further re-inforced by promoting the legal offer via awareness campaigns and the 'Youth Music Card' programme (though this has now ended).

While the HADOPI law technically has also created the ability for a 'notice and take down' approach to be used, this has only been used twice due to the perceived ineffectiveness of implementing this process in France.

Contextual Factors

As is common in European countries, France has a competitive market for broadband connections. Orange (formerly France Telecom) is the market leader with a market share of over 40%. The mature nature of the market is visible in the penetration rates that are in-line with the European standard: 37.8% in fixed connections and 52.2% in mobile for an overall total of 90%. Though France has a good position in terms of accessibility, network speeds are less competitive: according to Akamai, France has an average connection speed of 6.6 Mbit/s placing the country in a modest position worldwide (28th out of 55 countries). However, this is changing rapidly due to investment in optical fibre rollout and upgrades to the country's coaxial cable networks are ongoing. As an indication of the pace of change, at the end of September 2014, there were 2.5 million superfast broadband subscriptions in use, a growth of 34% in a year.[46]

In terms of online legal services, HADOPI identifies a thriving marketplace in online music, with 40 legal music providers operating in the country[47] and overall France is covered well by the main international players. In film all the three main players are present (Google Play, Netflix and iTunes) as in Music (Google Play, iTunes and Spotify) and although Google Play does not offer TV shows in France, iTunes does.

Since 2013, HADOPI has commissioned two waves of a representative survey, undertaken by Harris Interactive, that is used to develop a 'barometer' of the legal offer in France. This provides some quite detailed information regarding consumer awareness and rating of the legal offer. Reflecting a strong supply-side, awareness of the legal offer in music is quite high among French internet users (68%) and is also considered as easy to find (77% of users). In comparison, legal offers of TV series and films have slightly lower awareness (64% for both) and equally are also considered a bit harder to find (with 65% and 62% of users reporting that they consider legal offers in TV and movies easy to find respectively). Unsurprisingly, the survey shows that the preference for legal alternatives is not motivated by price. Instead, consumers report that the strengths of the legal offer for music lie in its technical quality, that it is easy to find, and that there are a variety of products and services. However, 75% of all consumers also identify illegal music offers as "easy to find". The overall attractiveness of legal music offering was noted by 62% of respondents, which is the same index of attractiveness for legal offers pictures, software and video games.

At the other end, TV series (57%) and films (56%) get the lowest ratings in terms of the attractiveness indices for their legal offer. These are also the two cultural product categories that are most likely to be consumed illegally, with 30% of users stating that they consume them via means that infringe copyright (either exclusively or partially), as compared to 23% for all digital cultural products.[48]

Background and Policy Process

The French online copyright enforcement strategy originates in the 2006 "Act for Copyright and Neighbouring Rights in the Information Society"[49] of the French legal system, which mandated the development of technical measures for online copyright enforcement. In 2007, the Minister of Culture and Communications, Christine Albanel, commissioned the CEO of FNAC (the largest entertainment retailer in France) to *"work towards concluding an agreement between professionals that allows for the development of appealing legal terms for online content and discourages widespread illegal downloading."*[50] This resulted in an agreement - signed by public authorities, copyright organisations and ISPs – which set forth provisions to establish specific legal and technical tools against online copyright infringement: the 'Agreement for the development and protection of cultural works and programmes on new networks' of 23 November 2007.

The agreement was followed by the drafting in 2008 of the "Hadopi 1 and 2" laws, which were to provide the main legislative and regulatory basis of the French online copyright infringement strategy. From October 2008 to October 2009, the French Parliament vehemently debated the draft bill of the "Hadopi 1 and 2" laws. Their legislative passage was extremely controversial and heavily covered by the media. The approach's punitive components, especially its ultimate legal penalty suspending users' internet access, were and have remained its most controversial and media-reported aspects. Such an emphasis on the punitive aspects of the laws has led to a widely shared lack of knowledge about their overall pedagogical function and the actual measures undertaken to combat infringement.

Legal and Regulatory Basis of Approach

The main legislation is the Hadopi 1, "law to encourage the distribution and protection of creative works on the Internet", which was passed on 12 June 2009[51], and Hadopi 2, "law on the legal protection of artistic and literary works on the Internet", passed on 28 October 2009[52]. The "Hadopi 1 and 2" laws re-affirm that internet subscribers are obligated to monitor their internet connections against acts of infringement committed through the use of P2P network software.[53]

While the "Hadopi 1 & 2" laws did not limit the scope of the graduated response to a specific uploading or downloading technique, a decree established in March 2010 on the automated processing of personal data by HADOPI only mentions acts of uploading and downloading committed via P2P networks[54]. Therefore, HADOPI is not legally allowed to process personal data for acts of infringement using uploading and downloading techniques other than P2P networking.

Finally, the Hadopi laws introduced an important article into the French Intellectual Property Code which gives copyright holders the opportunity to ask the French Courts to order any measures necessary to prevent or put an end to copyright infringements.[55] The order can be issued against any person or entity likely to aid or facilitate infringement (and thus against online intermediaries). This article has provided opportunities for copyright holders to issue 'notice and take down' actions to ISPs and search engines for sites that they believe to be hosting or enabling access to infringing content.[56]

Enforcement Process

Three key missions were conferred to HADOPI in the legislation: protect works against copyright infringement on "public online communications networks"; "promote the development of legal content services", and monitor "the legal and illegal use of works and objects subject to a copyright or neighbouring right on digital communications networks."[57] Under the first mandate, HADOPI is granted the power to identify internet subscribers associated with acts of infringement and to implement the graduated response procedure leading up to a gross negligence violation.

Graduated Response

Copyright owners, via audio-visual Collective rights Management Organisations (CMOs), are responsible for identifying acts of infringement and sending them to HADOPI. In practice, HADOPI has mostly processed citations from four audio-visual copyright organisations[58] and the HADOPI information system is networked with the systems at these four CMOs in order to receive their reports of copyright infringement.[59] The four CMOs were granted permission in 2007/2010 to use an automated processing system that provides search capabilities for acts of infringement on P2P networks and gathers the IP addresses of infringers, which are passed onto HADOPI. In order to do this, these copyright organisations have hired the private company Trident Media Guard (TMG), specialised in technical solutions against P2P illegal downloads.[60] Importantly, the system only records the IP addresses of infringers if they are based in France.[61] The CMOs then need to appoint sworn agents, accredited by the Ministry of Culture, to establish these listed infringements as legal claims before sending them to the HADOPI.

The ISPs are then responsible for identifying the subscribers behind acts of infringement. Once HADOPI has verified the admissibility and legality of the infringement claims it receives from copyright organisations, it sends subscriber identification requests to ISPs, which are obliged to disclose the information within eight days.

Once the ISP has identified the individual account and household that has been linked to the infringement, HADOPI sends the first of up to three notifications to the subscriber. Notifications contain information about existing legal penalties associated with online copyright infringement and information about responsible internet use and existing legal content offer. HADOPI sends new notifications for repeated offences. If the infringer has refused to curtail their activity, HADOPI forwards individual case files to the French Penal Courts when it decides that the pedagogical approach has been ineffective in stopping repeat offences.

- 1st notification: urging subscriber to meet the obligation to see that their Internet connection is not being used to commit an infringement, and to remind them of the penalties associated with the gross negligence violation;[62]
- 2nd notification: if acts of infringement are repeated within six months of the first notification being issued, HADOPI can send a second notification in the form of a recorded delivery letter. This second notification is one of the constitutive elements of the gross negligence violation; and
- 3rd notification: this begins if HADOPI receives information about new acts of infringement that are likely to constitute a gross negligence violation within one year of the date of the second notification. HADOPI assesses and reviews the case files to decide whether to forward it to the Attorney General (i.e. the French Penal Courts).

Subscribers are also invited in the notifications to contact and send remarks to HADOPI responding to the accusations. These remarks constitute very important elements of the ultimate deliberation by HADOPI as to whether to forward infringement case files to the French Penal Courts.

'Notice and Take Down'

One of the articles of the Hadopi laws has provided opportunities for copyright holders to issue 'notice and take down' actions to ISPs and search engines for sites that they believe to be hosting or enabling access to infringing content. Under this opportunity, audio-visual copyright organisations used legal means to impose on online intermediaries (both French ISPs and by extension search engines) the obligation to block 16 film streaming website domain names on November 18th 2013.[63] In 2014, the SCPP (Civil Society of Phonographic Producers) has entered into a legal procedure for French Courts to impose on online intermediaries the obligation to block access to 'The Pirate Bay' as well as its mirror and relay sites.[64]

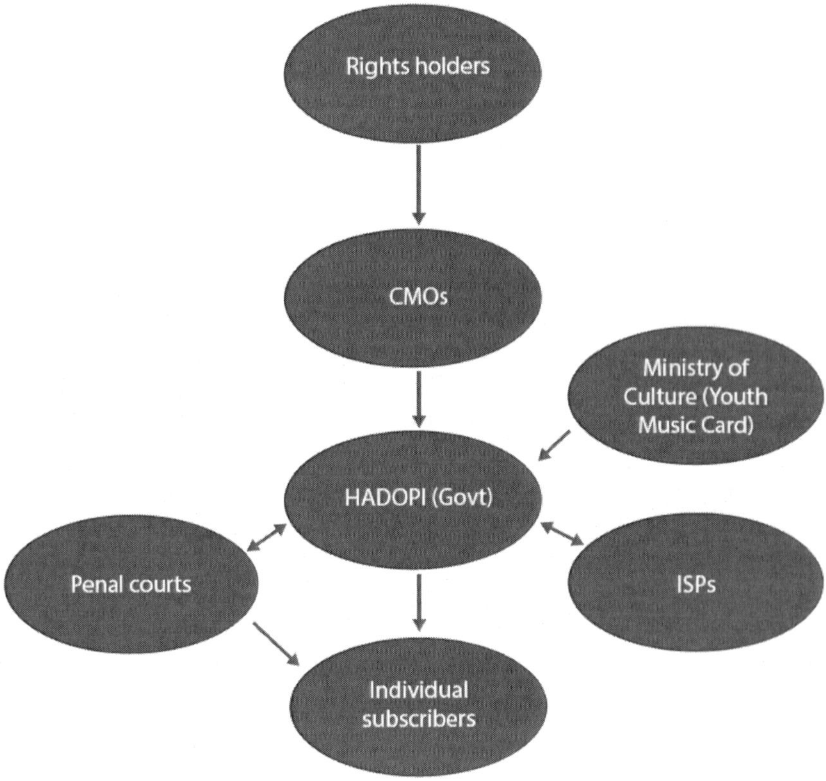

Source: BOP Consulting with DotEcon (2014).

Figure 11. Institutional configuration of the enforcement process in France.

Legal Offer Promotion

The third strand of French policy regarding copyright enforcement online has been to offer greater incentives to users to consume legal offerings. Specifically, between 2010 and 2012 the Ministry of Culture ran a 'Youth Music Card' programme: users aged between 12-25 years old users could buy a virtual card to purchase music on online legal platforms, whose initial cost value was then doubled with public match-funding. The 'Youth Music Card' programme had 14 online partners (including the most important legal online music stores in France such as Amazon, iTunes, Deezer and FNAC). In order to benefit from the initiative, 12-25 year old online consumers had to apply on the Youth Music Card's dedicated website, choose among a variety of legal platforms (with the option to mix between them), and obtain an identification code to use on these platforms. However, the scheme proved overly complex in its implementation, under subscribed and, as a result, closed in 2012.

Enforcement Measures / Sanctions

In association with the obligations of internet subscribers to monitor their internet connections, the "Hadopi 1 and 2" laws instituted a new infringement: the gross negligence violation, which carries a maximum penalty of a €1,500 fine (the previous additional sanction of the suspension of internet access for up to one month was overturned by decree in July 2013[65]).

Burden and Standard of Proof

As outlined above, claims from CMOs must first be verified by approved agents before they are forwarded to HADOPI. Claims from CMOs can only be admissible if they contain evidence against a range of criteria, including the date and time of the discovery; the P2P protocol used; information on the copyright-protected works and the file name; the subscriber's IP address on the date and at the time of the discovery; and any pseudonyms used on the peer-to-peer network[66].

Costs

The 2012 Bille Report attempted to evaluate the costs of the tools deployed as part of the French fight against online copyright infringement for the year 2011. While the figures this report advances for private stakeholders remain disputed ones, it is the most recent available study evaluating these costs over a one year period for all stakeholders involved. Not accounting for technical protection tools (such as DRM), the Bille Report estimated total costs borne by public stakeholders to represent between €23.3 million and €26 million (including activities promoting the legal offer), and the total costs to private actors to represent between €6.6 million and €7.9 million.

This worked out at an annual budget for HADOPI between 2010-12 of €11 million, 55% of which was dedicated to the graduated response scheme, and a €14.1 million annual subsidy from the Ministry of Culture for the 'Youth Music Card' programme during years of implementation. HADOPI's annual budget has since been reduced to €7 million in 2013-2014 (with 62% dedicated to graduated response), mostly as a result of not having to incur the sunk costs that were required during its first years of implementation. Estimates in the Bille Report of costs for rights holders related to implementing the graduated response scheme stood at €5.4 million in 2011, with the figure for ISPs estimated at between €1.2 million and €2.6 million in 2011 (though the government disputes these figures).

Implementation, Monitoring and Effectiveness

Graduated Response

HADOPI publishes monthly figures on the number of enforcement actions. The table below summarises the figures published by the HADOPI in July 2014.[67] The cumulative figures show that, while over 3m 1st stage notifications have been sent out, only about one tenth of these subscribers are found to have internet connections that have continued to be linked with infringing activity within the six months after receiving the first notification. In turn, less than one percent of those receiving a second stage notification receives the third and final notification.

	May 2014	Total cumulative since October 2010
# of 1st notification sent	149,357	3,249,481
# of 2nd notification sent	12,350	333,723
# of individual 3rd stage deliberations	71	1,289

In practice, only one subscription holder has been convicted with a suspension of his internet service since the creation of the Hadopi laws. The subscriber was convicted in June 2013 with a €600 fine and a 15-day suspension of his internet service. However, due to the July 2013 decree overturning the latter charge, his internet suspension penalty was revoked.[68] It is important to repeat here that the graduated response was principally designed as an educational measure. The HADOPI's deliberation process during the third stage of the graduated response is undertaken on a case-by-case basis taking into account the remarks one subscriber might have sent in response to the notifications and/or the measures one subscriber might have taken to monitor the connection against infringement (e.g. securing it). As a result, the ultimate deployment of legal penalties is not HADOPI's primary objective but only reserved for case files where the agency decides the pedagogical approach has been ineffective in stopping repeat offences. This has meant only a few case referrals to the legal system even for those receiving the third notification letter. [69]

Interestingly an independent study (Danaher et al., 2013/forthcoming[70]), which used data from four major record labels to analyse their sales on iTunes across five major European music markets, concludes that HADOPI has had a strongly positive impact on sales (+22%) when compared with the control group (Spain, Belgium, Germany, UK and Italy). However, there are a number of methodological limitations with the study that suggest that the effect might not have been as wholly positive as this in reality.[71]

'Notice and Take Down'

Copyright holders have only used this legal opportunity twice since the law made it possible in 2009. This is because 'notice and take down' actions in France remain largely ineffective under current legal conditions. First, rulings under this article do not specify the actions that ISPs and search engines must implement in order to comply with the terms of the decision, leaving it up to their interpretation. Second, there are currently no legal mechanisms in place for this blocking order to adapt to new site names, thus allowing websites containing infringing content to simply change their name once the court decision has been taken against them. Copyright holders still have to go via the French Courts if they wish to take down blocked sites that have changed their names, which can be an inordinately lengthy process when pitted against the speed of new online developments. Finally, orders have currently ruled that copyright holders were responsible for the costs of these blocking and filtering measures, which leaves them contemplating spending not insignificant amounts of money for an uncertain result.

ITALY

Overview of the Italian Approach

The Italian approach is two-fold:

1) In the first place, enforcement is conducted by both AGCOM, the Authority within the Italian Communication Sector, and the Guardia di Finanza (GdF) – translated as the 'Economic Police Body'. The two parties implement enforcement at different levels and in different ways. The GdF approach is active: the special department for technological fraud monitors and investigates copyright infringement. However they tend to concentrate on those instances of significant infringement, usually in the commercial realm (e.g. major piracy websites, such as commercial streaming and file hosting platforms). These crimes are then dealt with by the Italian penal court. AGCOM's approach, on the other hand, is reactive: the Authority only acts upon right holders requests and operates within the communication sector, hence through ISPs. The reactive nature of AGCOM's approach may change soon, as the possibility of adopting a more proactive approach is currently being discussed;[72] and
2) Secondly, Italy aims at increasing and facilitating access to legal online content. Confindustria Digitale, SIAE, AGCOM and other stakeholders in the sector seem to agree that amplifying the available legal content is a powerful solution to counteract infringement whilst retaining the benefits associated with the diffusion of creative content.[73] With this purpose, a Special Committee for the Promotion of the Legal Offer has recently been established. Given that the Committee is still in a start-up phase, its future strategy is also still being discussed.

Contextual Factors

According to a recent paper by AGCOM, the number of broadband connections in Italy is approximately 14 million, accounting for 68% of all internet connections.[74] The same study suggests that, in 2014, 44% of families have a fixed broadband line, which is considerably lower than the European average reported by Eurobarometer (65%).[75] Considering the ratio of fixed broadband connections per head the number decreases to 22%.[76] The spread of superfast broadband is also low: in Italy only 1% of the population has subscribed to a 'superfast' broadband connection so far: significantly less than the European average of 21%.[77] Mobile broadband connection is more widespread however: approximately 66% of the Italian population have access to a mobile broadband line, which is higher than the European average.[78] According to Akamai's 2014 *State of the Internet Report*, the average broadband speed is 5.2 Mbps/s, which places Italy relatively low down the rankings (33rd out of 55).

To date, no study has specifically sought to assess the level of access or the usage of legal digital content in Italy. However, a number of white papers as well as recent government communications has pointed to the urgent need to improve the digital offer and raise its awareness, as it still not yet suitable to provide an attractive alternative to infringing content.[79] According to Confindustria Digitale, online content is also still quite expensive, given that it is subject to VAT levied at 23%.[80] Further, access to legal digital content is also being hindered by the level of detail and information that consumers are required to provide in order to make an online purchase in Italy, such as having to input the equivalent of the National Insurance number.

However, there has been some progress in recent times, especially within the music sector. At present, there are 26 legal platforms offering digital music content in Italy, according to Pro Music. These include Spotify, which was finally launched in Italy in 2013 and generated 11 million streams within the first week.[81] According to a 2013 study carried out by the IFPI in collaboration to FIMI, the number of legal music downloads also increased at a rate of 25% between 2011 and 2012.[82] With regard to the film sector, both Google play and iTunes are available although it is not possible to comment on their usage due to the lack of available data. The major players in TV streaming (Google play, iTunes, and NetFlix) do not operate in Italy.

Background and Policy Process

Since the mid 2000s, online copyright infringement has grown steadily alongside Italy's broadband penetration. In common with many other countries, Italy first witnessed a rapid diffusion of P2P file sharing[83] and then also experienced the exponential growth of streaming and file hosting platforms. CD, SIAE and AGCOM agree that these commercial platforms hosting significant amounts of infringed content now constitute the greatest obstacle in the fight against infringement.[84]

Several studies have shown an exceptionally high level of piracy activity in Italy. While hard goods piracy levels are also high, the continued growth of internet piracy has become the primary concern for most copyright industries.85 [86] For instance, with regards to the videogame industry, in 2010 and 2011 the Entertainment Software Association (ESA) ranked Italy as first on the world scale for the number of connections by peers participating in unauthorized file sharing of select ESA member titles on public P2P networks.[87]

In light of the above, the growth of copyright infringement in Italy has become a cause for concern for the creative industries worldwide.[88] Between the years 2010 and 2013 Italy was repeatedly ranked amongst the worst countries with regard to online copyright infringement in several fields.[89] According to the International Intellectual Property Alliance (IIPA), the rapid spread of piracy in Italy was driven by two, inter-related factors. First, the high diffusion of piracy is due to a cultural factor: there is generally lax attitude towards the criminal nature of piracy both by users and by the courts. This consideration is backed by the findings of the aforementioned study conducted by FAPAV Ipsos, which found that 63% of interviewees deemed audio-visual piracy to be of little consequence although most of them were aware that it constitutes a crime.[90] Second, whilst Italy has certainly been active in adopting a suitable legal framework, it lacked enforcement resources such as specially designated process/courts. This resulted in a mismatch between the slow enforcement process on the one hand, and the rapid proliferation of piracy on the other end.

Nevertheless, as highlighted by AGCOM and CD, most of the data collected about infringing activity in Italy has been collected by actors in the industry who have a clear business interest in demonstrating the negative effects of piracy. Increased access to creative content resulting from the diffusion of online material can also bring positive effects to the economy - opportunities for information, education and familiarisation with technology. The challenge then, has been to maintain the same level of access to creative content whilst simultaneously respecting rights holders. This has been problematic in Italy as legal services have been very slow to be established in the country: Spotify, for instance, was not launched in Italy until 2013.[91]

Hence, most of the institutions in the sector agree about the need to develop a legal framework which allows for a more efficient and effective enforcement system whilst simultaneously fostering access to legal online content through increasing and promoting the legal offer. These two objectives stand as the basis of the new AGCOM regulation, approved in December 2013, and implemented in March 2014.

Legal and Regulatory Basis of Approach

The Italian Copyright Act (Law 22nd April 1941, n. 633) and AGCOM Online Copyright Regulation (12th December, 2013, n. 680/13/CONS) constitute the main basis of the Italian legal framework within the online copyright realm. Whilst AGCOM new regulation has just been established, the Italian Copyright Act has been updated with specific rules by several legislative decrees throughout the 2000s to incorporate specific rules regarding copyright.

Enforcement Process

According to AGCOM, Online Copyright Regulation (2013) rights holders are responsible for identifying infringement, although the GdF also unilaterally investigates instances of major piracy, such as streaming platforms.

If a rights holder becomes aware of infringing activity, they have two options:

- Report it to AGCOM: if the claim of the copyright holders is deemed admissible, AGCOM notifies it to the appropriate ISPs, to the uploader and to the Webpage and Website Managers, who are to disable access to the infringed content. ISPs can either comply with AGCOM order or raise exceptions. If the ISP fails to comply with AGCOM's order to disable access to the infringed content they can face substantial fines. The whole procedure ranges from 12 days (super fast procedure) to 35 days (standard procedure). A new online platform, run by the Fondazione Ugo Bordoni (a CMO) has been designed as the system through which rightsholders requests are channelled to AGCOM; and
- Report it to the Guardia di Finanza (GdF). AGCOM acts upon right holders' requests and orders ISPs to selectively remove access to infringed content whereas the GdF concentrates on actively pursuing

major piracy cases (e.g. illegal commercial streaming and file hosting platforms).

It should be stressed that the GdF also proactively targets what it considers to be major illegal activity, regardless of whether a rights holders has first come forward to instigate an action. This proactive initiative does not just focus on content providers and enablers. Rather, the GdF takes a ‘follow the money’ approach and also targets any advertising or financial intermediaries that are transacting with illegal sites.

Finally, the Italian government aims to increase and facilitate access to legal online content. With this purpose, a Special Committee for the Promotion of Legal Offer has recently been established by the new AGCOM regulation.

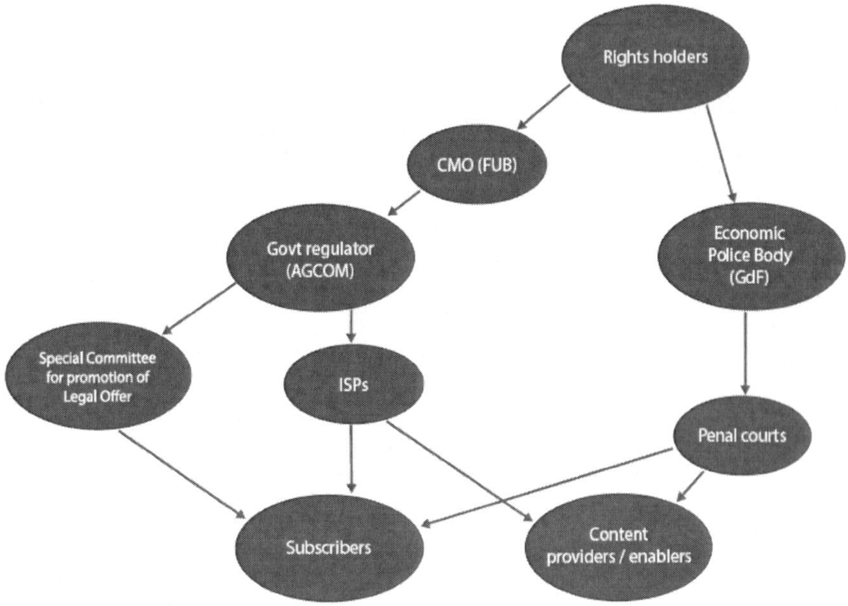

Source: BOP Consulting with DotEcon (2014).

Figure 12. Institutional configuration of the enforcement process in Italy.

Enforcement Measures / Sanctions

According to article 171 of the Italian Copyright Act, anyone who without authorization "makes a copyright work or part thereof available to the public by entering it into a system of telematic networks (i.e., the Internet), through connections of any kind" including those who are not doing it for commercial purpose can be fined-although those who commit such acts for commercial gains are punished more severely. Downloaders of infringed content can also be sanctioned, though these are not the main focus of enforcement measures. The new AGCOM Online Copyright regulation aims primarily at disabling access to infringed material, operating through ISPs. ISPs which fail to comply with AGCOM orders will face fines from EUR 10,000 to 250,000 (this fine applies in any instance in which ISPs fail to comply and is not copyright specific).

Burden and Standard of Proof

When contacting AGCOM copyright holders must fill in an online form, which requires, amongst other details, to clearly state the work that has been infringed, and the web location in which the infringement is taking place. This relatively easy procedure is in line with AGCOM objective of making copyright protection accessible to everyone. Right holders on the other hand can also denounce the infringement to the penal courts. In the latter case the standard of proof will depend upon several factors including the volume and consistency of infringement.

Costs

The costs of implementation for the new AGCOM regulation are estimated to be €535,000 spread over three years (2014, 2015, 2016). This covers the management of the new online platforms through which the Fondazione Ugo Bordoni, on behalf of AGCOM, will collect right holders' requests and direct them to the appropriate ISPs[92]. These and all additional costs will be covered by ISPs. This is because AGCOM is entirely financed by ISPs, who give out 0.2% of their income to AGCOM[93]. As such, ISPs not only cover the costs of identifying the infringed content and selectively removing access to it, but they also cover the cost of processing rights holder's requests submitted to AGCOM. According to CD the distribution of the cost has not been discussed and it is likely to remain unchanged in the future[94]. On the other hand, SIAE may start contributing to cover some of the costs entailed by the procedure in the future[95]. With regards to the GdF and the penal courts it is not clear how much exactly is currently being spent on dealing with online copyright. The GdF reports their allocated costs are approximately £640,000 per year, however there is no estimate for how much is spent by the penal courts.

Implementation, Monitoring and Effectiveness

AGCOM's new regulations have been implemented since March 2014. The Special Committee (article 4) is currently working towards developing a viable strategy in order to increase and facilitate access to the legal offer. The Special Committee is also in the process of identifying an effective monitoring and evaluation strategy. Given the recent implementation, it is still too early to assess the effectiveness of the new regulation. However, according to AGCOM there has been a 100% positive response from ISPs so far. With regards to the enforcement measures undertaken by the GdF, there is currently no monitoring in place to assess the impact or the effectiveness of the enforcement.

The Netherlands

Overview of the Dutch Approach

Dutch copyright policy approach is based on the government providing a legal framework within which private parties operate to protect their copyright. Enforcement efforts focus on content providers (supply), not on consumers of content (demand). The legal framework has been supplemented with a Code of Conduct that regulates a great deal of the activities from rights holders in the protection of their rights. The procedures intend to facilitate private parties (rights holders, ISPs, content providers) to deal with infringement between themselves, outside of the judicial system. This approach has been influenced by the fact that, up until a ruling by the European Court of Justice on 10th April 2014, downloading copyrighted material without compensation by private citizens was not illegal in the

Netherlands – this is no longer the case after the court ruling. However, despite this, the focus of enforcement will remain the supply of unlawful content, not on individual downloaders / demand, at least in the short term.

In addition to the voluntary Notice and Take Down procedures, the anti-piracy foundation of rights holders and artists (BREIN) also take other actions to tackle infringement. This can be summarised as a 'follow the money' approach that targets financial intermediaries (e.g. Pay Pal and banks) and advertisers (or intermediaries that link advertisers to the sites) to request them to refrain from transacting with sites that infringe copyright, as well as Google (to get them to take down search results that link to infringing sites).

Contextual Factors

Internet access is a foremost concern in the economic policy of the Netherlands. The Netherlands was the second country in the world to enact a net neutrality law, indicating the importance of internet in the development of government policy. The Netherlands is also one of the few countries not to enact broadband caps. All of which has combined to make the Netherlands one of the most competitive countries in the digital economy with a broadband penetration (measured as number of accounts) that exceeds 100% (100.4%) with 61% in mobile and 39.4% in fixed.

In terms of the legal offer, data from Pro-Music shows the availability of 32 legal online music providers in the Netherlands.[96] All the major players are available in the country for both music and film, although film and TV have lagged behind music. Indeed, a study commissioned by the Ministry of Economic Affairs in 2012 concluded that, while the country had a comprehensive and competitive legal offer for music, the film and TV industries' strategy of windowing and the greater trouble clearing rights for multi territories meant that the audio-visual market was still fragmented and incomplete.[97] However, the situation has changed significantly since, with foreign content providers such as Netflix and HBO Go, as well as domestic content providers such as NLZiet and Videoland Unlimited, all entering the Dutch market. Further support to promote legal online services has been given by the Ministry of Education, Culture and Science and the Federation of Copyright Holders, who jointly launched www.thecontentmap.nl with links to all the legal online providers of music, films and television programs, games, e-books, images and animation.

Although there has been no formal tracking surveys run of online copyright infringement levels, two cross sectional studies undertaken by the same authors provide some interesting insight into the changing marketplace in The Netherlands.[98] The survey-based studies suggest that the share of consumers that pay to download or stream films has risen substantially: from 11.8 percent in May 2012 to 20 percent in January 2014. This figure is only slightly less than the proportion of consumers who had consumed at least one film via an illegal stream or download (28%), although the average number of films consumed illegally was more than four times greater than the average for legal streaming or downloading. While the free cost was the overwhelming reason given for consuming copyright content online in ways that infringe copyright (68%), again, timeliness was the second most important factor ('don't want to wait for the film to be shown in the cinema',36%).

Background and Policy Process

In the past two decades the Netherlands has developed one of the best and most competitive digital infrastructures in the world.[99] A good infrastructure and a competitive market tend to produce favourable prices and, since the first years of the millennium, this led to the Netherlands gaining a large share of the site hosting market. The large capacity and low price of internet hosting in the country not only attracted websites with legal content, but also a large number of sites that were totally or partially directed at providing unlawful content.

In the first decade of the millennium, conflict arose over the legality of hosting sites with unlawful content in the Netherlands[100]. The clashes were not only fought out in court, but also in the public arena: opinions from those advocating the necessity to compensate rights holders and to prevent piracy (such as those expressed by BREIN), were opposed by views from parties that stressed the danger of censorship and the need for privacy.[101] After a few years of continuous confrontation, a certain form of consensus was established about what was acceptable and what not. Part of the path to consensus was the development and agreement of the Noticeand-Take-Down Code of Conduct[102] that was established in 2008 by a number of public and private organisations, operating together in the National Infrastructure against Cybercrime.

The NTD Code describes a procedure for intermediaries (aka ISPs) to deal with reports of unlawful content on the Internet[103]. It has a broader scope than just copyright and intellectual property as it also covers matters such as the distribution of child pornography, racist statements, defamatory expressions, cyberstalking and the violation of people's privacy by publishing personal data. The Code establishes no new statutory obligations, but intends to help organisations to operate carefully within the existing legislative framework regarding the removal of information from the Internet at the request of third parties. Complying with the NTD Code is voluntary and there is no formal enforcement in the case of non-compliance. The benefits of complying with the NTD Code lie in the achievement of more efficient procedures and in the reduction of liability risks. The NTD Code intends to contribute to the ability of private individuals and organisations to deal effectively with these types of reports between themselves wherever possible. If this fails, there always remains the possibility to bring a matter before the courts or to report a case officially to the police.

Recent Developments

On April 10th, 2014 the EU Court of Justice ruled in a case[104] with direct consequences for the Dutch approach to online copyright infringement. The key outcome of the case was that the Dutch government interpreted the ruling of the EU Court of Justice in such a way that from that moment downloading from an illegal source was no longer lawful in the Netherlands. This was stated in a letter from the Dutch government to Parliament, one week after the ruling.[105] Theoretically the ruling could have far-reaching consequences. Until April 10th 2014, private citizens could fearlessly download copyrighted material from an illegal source. After the EU Court ruling, the same activity had suddenly become unlawful and could therefore lead to prosecution. The chances of that happening however seem very limited, with rights holders publicly stating that the target of enforcement measures remained unchanged: "illegal shops on the internet, not downloading individuals."[106]

Legal and Regulatory Basis of Approach

Policy is based on the Copyright Act 1912[107] and the Neighbouring Rights Act 1993.[108] The Copyright Act has been amended almost every year, but arguably the most significant recent change was in 2004, to comply with the European directive regarding the harmonisation of copyright and neighbouring rights in the European Union (2001/29/EG European Parliament and the European Council (May 21, 2001). However, as outlined above, the main way in which enforcement is tackled is through voluntary processes that are supported via the NTD Code of Conduct.

Enforcement Process

At the national level, three different ministries cooperate in formulating intellectual property policy: the Ministry of Security and Justice, the Ministry of Education, Culture and Science, and the Ministry of Economic Affairs. The Ministry of Security and Justice takes the lead in terms of policy formulation. In addition, the Public Prosecutor's Office can decide to prosecute parties that are suspected of infringing copyright[109], and private parties can summon suspected infringers before a civil court.[110]

The Copyright Act and the Neighbouring Rights Act specify which acts should be considered as infringements and which sanctions are applicable. Involved parties can bring these issues before a civil or criminal court, but the law does not specify how these cases should be handled outside of court. This is where the NTD Code of Conduct comes into play as it specifies the steps parties should take to tackle infringements outside of the judicial system. The Code describes the order of steps to be taken and offers escalation options if prior steps fail to solve the conflict. In brief, the steps are as follows:

- Rights holders ('the notifier') report alleged unlawful content;
- The notifier first tries to contact the content provider directly;
- If direct contact does not succeed, the notifier contacts the intermediary (i.e. the ISP);
- Intermediary evaluates the reported claim of unlawful content (if the rights holder is represented by a professional notifier, evaluation by the ISP is not necessary); and
- If the conflict is not solved in this way, the rights holder can bring the case to civil court.

An important obstacle in the application of the Code in the Dutch practice is the fact that content providers can remain anonymous[111], or be located abroad and therefore outside of the jurisdiction of Dutch laws and regulations. In these cases, the notifier can request intermediaries to block access to unlawful content, which brings the ISP into conflict in its role as an access provider, not as a hosting provider.

According to BREIN, 99% of the sites they start to research because of suspected infringement operate anonymously. In most cases BREIN does not succeed in identifying the organisation or person that runs the site. The next step, as described above, is to turn to the hosting provider. If the suspected unlawful content is well documented and the hosting service is delivered within the Netherlands, the site can be taken down in a matter of days. Because BREIN is a trusted partner, the ISP refrains from reviewing the case and acts immediately. On average the take down takes 2 to 5 days.

If BREIN does succeed in identifying the suspected infringer, which happens in about one in five of all cases, several options are open. The first is to try and reach a settlement, and a well-documented file in combination with available jurisprudence makes for a strong case. According to BREIN, settlement is reached in the majority of cases where they can identify the party giving access to unlawful material: the infringer agrees to take the unlawful material down and to 'stay down'. A penalty applies if the infringer does not comply with the settlement. In some cases the settlement also covers the compensation the infringer agrees to pay to the rights holders for the damage done (enforcement costs and/or lost income).

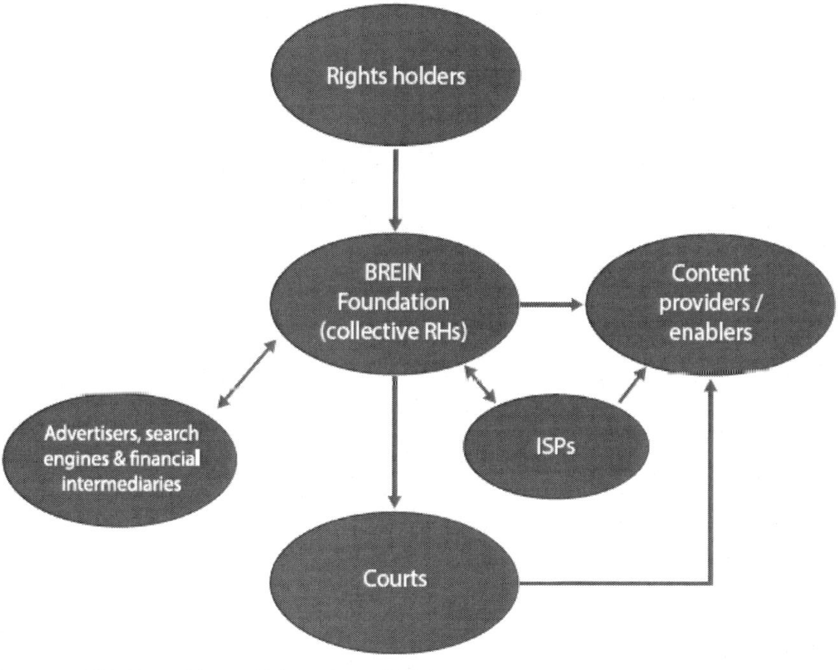

Source: BOP Consulting with DotEcon (2014).

Figure 13. Institutional configuration of the enforcement process in the Netherlands.

Enforcement Measures / Sanctions

If the voluntary process suggested within the Code fails to produce a satisfactory resolution, then all parties concerned can bring the dispute about alleged unlawful content before a civil court. In particular, the rights holder or their representative can ask for a preliminary injunction. If the plaintiff wins the case, the site has to be taken down immediately and the defendant can be convicted to pay all costs of litigation (somewhere between €8.000 to €15.000). A preliminary injunction is a quick way to settle, but does not include the possibility of compensation. To request for compensation, a much longer procedure has to be followed. Additionally the sanctions mentioned in the Copyright Act that could be pursued are as follows:[112]

- Article 31 states that he who intentionally infringes another's copyright, shall be punished with imprisonment with a maximum of six months or a fine of € 20,250;[113]
- Article 31a states that if the copyrighted work is offered for distribution, reproduction, is imported or exported or stored for profit, shall be punished with imprisonment with a maximum of one year or a fine of € 81,000; and
- Article 31b states that he who makes his profession of the offences mentioned in Articles 31 and 31a, shall be punished with imprisonment with a maximum of four years or a fine of € 81,000.

Burden and Standard of Proof

The notifier needs to document the nature and content of the infringement. Neither the NTD Code of Conduct, nor its explanatory notes, contain provisions regarding the burden of proof in the report of a notifier. The standard of proof is therefore determined by law and jurisprudence.

Costs

One of the rationales behind the Dutch approach is the desire not to burden the judicial system with conflicts that can be solved elsewhere, with the legal system only acting as a fall back option. The lack of dedicated structures and processes within central government also means that costs related to copyright enforcement are kept to a minimum. The bulk of the costs thereby fall on the rights holders and ISPs in terms of the time spent identifying and negotiating resolutions in each case. None of the costs attributable to the different parties are publicly available.

Implementation, Monitoring and Effectiveness

As BREIN is the main actor in the field of online infringement of intellectual property, they provide a fairly comprehensive picture of the Dutch practice of enforcement. In their annual report[114] BREIN presents the following results for 2013:

- 510 sites were taken offline and just a few of these sites did not operate anonymously. The majority were taken offline after reports to the intermediary (i.e. the ISP).
- 1 site (The Pirate Bay) was blocked by ISPs and 206 proxies were removed that tried to circumnavigate the access block to The Pirate Bay;
- In 41 cases, payment providers provided BREIN with information to identify illegal sites and stopped servicing the operators of these sites. More than 100 advertisers also committed to stop advertising on sites propagating the unlawful supply of films, series, music, books and games;
- At the request of BREIN, Google also removed more than 2.3 million search results to illegal files; and
- Finally, BREIN software made more than 10 thousand cyberlocker files inaccessible, and the foundation removed more than 14 thousand files at cyberlockers and 1,500 on YouTube.

In view of the progress made in the Netherlands, stakeholders that were interviewed agree that Dutch enforcement policy has been successful over the past few years. An important contribution has been made by the right holders working together in BREIN: their efforts have led to a decline in the hosting of websites with unlawful content or with links to unlawful content (as outlined above in relation to action carried out in 2003).

However, problems still remain. Firstly, the Netherlands continues to be one of the top countries for the location of sites engaged in wider cybercrimes (e.g. the hosting of phishing and spam urls[115]). More germane to the issue of copyright infringement, the success of Dutch enforcement policy has meant that the organisations that provide unlawful material from within the Netherlands are now either small and specialised or unaware of their infringement. This is because the larger scale websites that enable access to unlawful content have fled Dutch jurisdiction and moved to other countries.

As a result of this trend, the focus of enforcement now includes unlawful content that is hosted outside of Dutch jurisdiction but that is consumed (downloaded, streamed) within the Netherlands. However, there is less consensus between parties with regard to this, and it is currently the subject of a four-year court battle between BREIN and two ISPs (XS4all and Ziggo). The terms of the debate are essentially the same as ever: the necessity to compensate right holders on the one hand and to prevent unlawful actions versus net neutrality, the danger of censorship and the need for privacy protection on the other - but this time with the addition from the ISPs that a blockade of 'offshore' sites is also not effective.[116]

SOUTH KOREA

Overview of the South Korean approach

The South Korean approach does not distinguish between whether copyright infringement is undertaken by individual subscribers or by online content providers/sites that enable access to infringing content: both are the focus of enforcement efforts. The 2009 revision of the South Korea Copyright Act gave the Ministry of Culture, Sport and Tourism (MCST) a range of new powers to combat online infringement, including a 'notice and take down' approach for content providers as well as an effective 'notice and desist' to individual subscribers. These measures are implemented as a graduated response process, consisting of a three stage warning. Extra judicial sanctions that can be taken by MCST under the Act focus on the termination of internet access for up to six months; rights holders can also choose to pursue infringers through the courts, where conviction could result in relatively heavy fines or imprisonment. Unlike France's graduated response system, South Korea's has resulted in a high number of cases being passed to the Public Prosecutor General for consideration. Alongside these punitive measures, the public-private Copyright Protection Centre has launched a preventative initiative (the 'Clean Sites Project') which publicises and signposts the legal offer.

South Korea is more pro-active in identifying copyright infringement than any other country in the study, with the task of identification not only falling to rights holders. Rather, identification is the active responsibility of a number of different state and quasi-state actors, and even the general public, through a 'netizen' reporting system (the 'Open Monitoring System'). However, the downside of having so many institutions engaged in tackling online copyright infringement has been a degree of overlap, duplication and fragmentation in the process. For this reason, the South Korean government is reviewing the current institutional arrangements and consolidating them into a new Copyright Protection Board.

Contextual Factors

As noted above in the 'Background and context section', the internet and the digital economy are strategic government priorities in South Korea and the country usually ranks high in terms of accessibility, penetration and broadband speeds. Indeed, the Akamai 2014 *State of the Internet* report places South Korea firmly ahead in terms of having the fastest average broadband connection speed in the world, by a wide margin: 23.6 Mbit/s compared with 14.6 Mbit/s in Japan in second place. In terms of penetration, the number of broadband mobile accounts outnumbers the actual population, making the effective penetration rate for mobile alone 106%. The total broadband coverage (mobile and fixed) stands at 143.6%, behind only Singapore (149.4%).

The analysis of legal alternatives by the major international players is likely to be a bit misleading in the case of South Korea as they tend to be western-oriented and ergo have a lower relevance in Asia. Nevertheless, according to Pro-Music, South Korea still has 17 legal online music services, despite the three big players in music (Google Play, iTunes and Spotify) not operating in the country. Moreover, the South Korean Copyright Protection Centre, runs a 'Clean Index' of legal sites and currently there are 51 legal online content services that have met the designation.

Background and Policy Process

Since coming to office in 2013, President Park Geun-hye has adopted the slogan of 'Creative Economy' for South Korea's overarching economic policy agenda. The phrase 'Culture-centred Creative Economy Era' has become prevalent in both policy and popular discourses. One of Park administration's proposed keynote national agenda is 'cultural prosperity'[117], which highlighted a healthy ecosystem for the copyright industry[118] as its basis. In turn, the South Korean government adopted the 'protection of intellectual property right and establishment for fair trade order' as one of the key national issues and has since been robustly implementing copyright protection policies.

However, in addition to being part of a wider domestic, innovation-led industrial policy, rapid institutional developments regarding copyright protection policy in recent years were also partly motivated by efforts to be taken off of the U.S. Trade Representative (USTR)'s Watch List countries in 2008. It should be noted in passing that the measures taken by South Korea have been successful: South Korea has not featured on the USTR Watch List for six straight years since 2009.

The main legal basis for tackling copyright infringement in South Korea is the Copyright Act. Since the original Copyright Act of 1957, the Act has had 14 amendments, including two consolidations (1986, 2006), and has gradually become more restrictive, especially over the last five years. The 2009 revision of the Act is the most substantial thus far, as it gave the Ministry of Culture, Sports and Tourism (MCST) and the South Korean Copyright Commission (KCC) the power to delete illegal reproductions, warn copyright infringers and to suspend their online access, through a three strikes policy.

The identification of infringement first targeted the most popular technology for infringing in South Korea (a form of file sharing software called 'Webhards'), but has subsequently moved to monitoring P2P networks as the nature of infringement has evolved over time (possibly in response to the regulatory crackdown on Webhards).

Institutional Configuration

The copyright protection system in South Korea comprises the public sector - consisting of MCST and the South Korea Copyright Commission (KCC); the Copyright Protection Centre, a unique public-private initiative between the MCST and the South Korean CMOs, and the CMOs themselves, 11 of which are registered under the South Korea Federation of Copyright Organizations (KOFOCO)).

Additionally, MCST has established the Copyright Special Judicial Police (CSJP). The CSJP are based in five regional centers in major cities (Seoul, Busan, Gwangju, Daejeon and Daegu), and are in charge of crackdowns and investigation into copyright infringement cases in their respective jurisdictions. MCST also introduced a Digital Copyright Forensics Team in 2010 to advance criminal investigations of those thought likely to be engaging in copyright infringement for the purposes of making money.

The South Korea Copyright Commission operates an online piracy reporting portal website (www.copy1112.or.kr) for receiving complaints on online piracy lodged by rights holders (or the general public) and for issuing correction recommendations based on these complaints. Since 2011, the KCC has also operated a national Open Monitoring System (OMS) through which the general public ('netizens') can directly report websites distributing illegal content. It is thought to be particularly useful for identifying infringement where external monitoring is more difficult, for instance for closed Webhards, on blogs and within communities. During the pilot period in 2011, 13,204 complaints were reported and the OMS is now a part of the overall KCC copyright protection portal, 'copy112'. The OMS runs a monthly point incentives program, awarding coupons and gift cards to top reporters of infringement, with an annual value upper limit of KRW 3 million (approx. £1,730) per person.[119]

The Copyright Protection Centre (CPC) utilizes a technical system, the Illegal Copyrights Obstruction Project (ICOP)[120] system to automatically search and gather evidence of illegal reproductions. They then send requests to suspend the reproduction and transmission of any infringed content to the content providers/enablers. In 2013, the technology was enhanced to include BitTorrent-related sites. The ICOP system is run via the Disabled Home Monitoring Project, which uses home-bound people with disabilities to run ICOP and monitor for infringements 24 hours a day. After a trial period, the Disabled Home Monitoring Project was scaled up to 350 employees.

On the preventative front, the CPC has also run the 'Copyright Clean Website List' since 2009 for the content providers/enablers, and has established a 'Clean Index' after consultations with industry and legal professionals and academics. Content Providers can apply for their sites to be designated by the Copyright Protection Centre, which involves review by an expert panel based on a 'Clean Index' and 'Legal Service Guidelines'. Currently there are 51 designated 'clean sites' and the number has been increasing at a rapid annual rate (52%).

Legal and Regulatory Basis of the Approach

The basis for enforcement action is legislation in the form of The Copyright Act. Since the original Copyright Act of 1957, the Act has undergone amendments 20 times, including two consolidations in 1986 and 2006. The 2009 amendment of the Act is perhaps the most substantial thus far, as it gave the Ministry of Culture, Sports and Tourism (MCST) and the South Korean Copyright Commission (KCC)[121] the power to delete illegal reproductions, warn copyright infringers via athree strikes process and to suspend their internet access. TheTelecommunications Business Act was also revised in November 2011 to restrict illegal transfer activities through Webhards, by enforcing the 'Webhard Registration System' (WRS).

Enforcement Process

As outlined above, the identification of online infringement is the joint responsibility of the MCST, the KCC and the CPC. In practice, it is also supported by copyright holders themselves and by the general public ('netizens'). Whoever identifies the infringement, the processes are the same:

- Extra judicial process: MCST can authorise the collection, disposal or deletion of illegal reproductions or devices / equipment / information / programmes from content providers and ISPs. If content providers/enablers that receive a 'correction order' and they do not carry out the actions (i.e. take down and deletion), they can be fined up to KRW 10 million (approx. £5,770). If an individual subscriber has received three or more warnings, MCST may order the relevant ISP to suspend their internet account for a set period of up to 6 months. If a content provider/enabler has received orders of deletion or suspension of transmission more than three times, then MCST can order the suspension of the entire or partial service for a set period of up to 6 months; and
- Judicial process: if there is an injunction claim by the copyright holder or prosecution of a criminal case in accordance with the Copyright Act, the court (via the Public Prosecutor General) may order the ISP to terminate special accounts or to take reasonable actions in order to block access to specific foreign internet sites. The court may also order deletion of illegal reproductions, deny access to illegal copies

and terminate relevant accounts held with the ISP. If found convicted, infringers may additionally face hefty fines or a prison sentence (as outlined below).

At every stage of this process, content providers/enablers and subscribers are given the opportunity to submit a statement to defend their actions, though this must be submitted to MCST within a short timeframe.

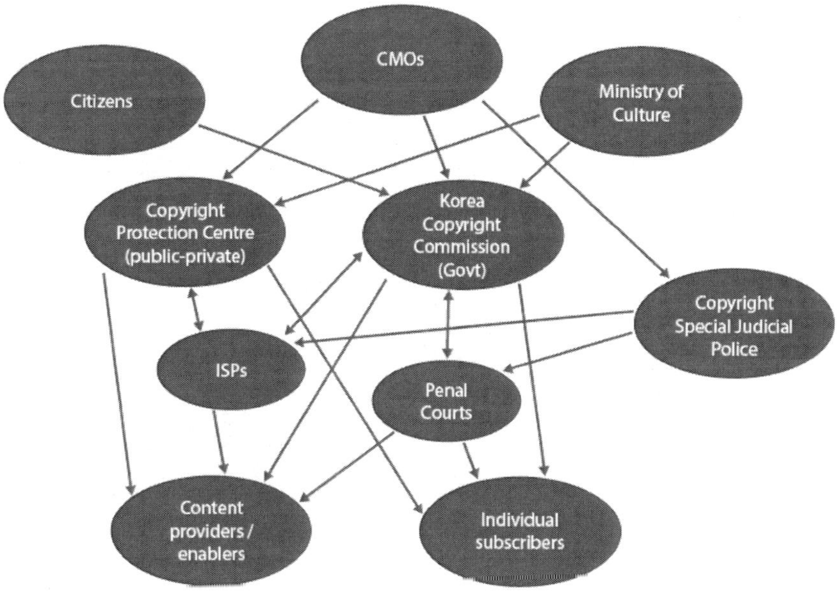

Source: BOP Consulting with DotEcon (2014).

Figure 14. Institutional configuration of the enforcement process in South Korea.

Enforcement Measures / Sanctions

The extra judicial process which MCST leads focuses upon deletion and blocking of sites and suspension of internet access. If a case proceeds to court, any person who infringes upon the economic rights of an author or a performer etc. may be subject to imprisonment for up to five years, or a fine of up to KRW 50 million (approx. £28,000) or both. Any person who infringes upon a creator's moral rights may be subject to imprisonment for up to three years or a fine of up to KRW 30 million or both.[122]

Burden and Standard of Proof

With regard to the extra judicial process, the deliberation of individual cases is carried out by the expert group of the South Korea Copyright Commission (KCC). As the KCC is also one of the agencies that identifies cases of infringement and prosecutes claims, it functions as both policeman and judge.

Costs

MCST incurs the costs of monitoring and identifying infringement. The 2013 MCST budget designated for copyright protection enhancement-related costs were KRW 13 billion (approx. £7.5million)[123]. MCST also covers the annual operational cost of the KCC - KRW 9 billion (approx. £5.2million). The cost of the CPC, as a private entity, is additional to these sums.

Implementation, Monitoring and Effectiveness

As the responsibility for enforcing copyright is split across a number of different bodies, the statistics are fragmented.

- Since 2009, the KCC has published statistics on the number of correction notifications it has issued annually. In its first year, it issued 85,085 recommendations rising to 250,039 in 2012, which were split mainly between 'warnings' (130,304) and 'deletion' or blocking (119,560). Only 175 notifications led to account suspension; and
- Judicial action: in 2013, just over 3,000 cases were indicted, with 2 individuals given prison sentences. Over 7,500 people had their indictment suspended and over 6,500 people had their indictments dismissed.

In addition to the monitoring of the number of actions taken against infringers, the Copyright Protection Centre conducts annual surveys of the public to investigate the 'Distribution of Illegal Reproductions'. Based on survey data, CPC's most recent estimates for 2013 suggest that 33% of the South Korean population, in the 13-69 age group, have consumed one of more work copyrighted work in a way that infringed copyright.[124] However, according to their annual estimates, the proportion of people who are engaged in some form of infringement has fallen from 54% in 2008 to 30.7% in 2013. As with other surveys of this nature, no attempt has been made to identify any confounding factors, such as the penetration of legal offerings, in the analysis.

SPAIN

Overview of the Spanish Approach

The current framework of enforcement in Spain does not focus on the demand-side (i.e. individual users and internet subscribers) but on the hosts of what is perceived to be illegal content, and more recently, advertisers that use such sites.

This was initiated through new legislation – what is commonly known as *Ley Sinde*[125], 2009, which became effective on December 2011, and a current revision that is in place known as *Ley Lassale*. The legislation created the Comission de Propriedad Intelectual (the Intellectual Property Commission) with the mission to identify if a specific webpage infringes established copyright. The new powers allow rights holders to report specific websites that infringe their copyright to the IPC. Once the request is approved the owner of the website must take down the material. If the owner of the website is not known, this request can be made through the ISP.

Contextual Factors

Spain has a modern infrastructure in telecommunications: ADSL internet was introduced in 1999. The current infrastructure is led by Telefonica, a public company based in Spain, considered to be the 7th largest mobile network operator in the world. Like most advanced economies, Spain has a high penetration of broadband (total 77.5% of the population), both in fixed (24%) and mobile (53%). However, the country performs worse when speed of connection is taken into account. In the latest Akamai *State of the Internet Report* (2014), the average speed of broadband connection in Spain is 7.2 Mbit/s, placing it 27th in the world (out of 55) and 19th in Europe.

Spain is often considered the worst offender in Western Europe when analysing online copyright infringement (see below), yet the number of legal alternatives in Spain has grown in the last couple of years. The analysis of data from Pro-Music suggests that 28 legal online music services are available in Spain, including the major international players (iTunes, Google Play and Spotify). However, Netflix does not operate in Spain and this reflects a wider gap related to the availability of legal alternatives for TV content, which none of the major players (Google Play, iTunes and Netflix) provide in Spain. As a predominantly non-English speaking country, Spain faces the limitation that the availability of local content is going to be very limited across the major international providers of legal online audio-visual services. This omission might be particularly relevant as the Spanish language market is several times greater than the Spanish market itself (i.e. the country).

Background and Policy Process

"Ley Sinde" (the Sinde law) was named after Ángeles González-Sinde, the Minister of Culture. This piece of legislation was part of a wider legislation project known as the Sustainable Economy Act. This legislation gained some unexpected media attention after the diplomatic cables published by Wikileaks[126] – it was revealed that the US government through its Madrid embassy pressured the Spanish government towards more strict legislation based on the US's own Stop Online Piracy Act (SOPA), which would be more in line with the strategic stance of the US government. This political pressure arose because for several years Spain had been classified in the 301 Special Report[127] as a 'priority country'. While the US government can place trade restrictions on countries included in the 301 list, as a full WTO member Spain would be immune to such a decision. But the possibility was there for the lack of legislation and policy action regarding online copyright enforcement to become at least a point of public embarrassment for Spain in international trade agreements, if not a full blown diplomatic problem with the US.

Access to illegal copyright material in Spain is widespread. Several pieces of different research point out Spain as the worst offender in Western Europe. IDC research suggests that almost all music consumption is derived illegally (98%). Significant levels of infringement is strongly suggested by the sales of CDs, which declined from 71 million in 2001 to only 10 million in 2010. The same source identifies 77% of movie downloads and 61% of game downloads as illegal. The report estimates the total cost of online piracy in Spain at €5.2bn (£4.3bn) – though it should be noted that this study was commissioned by La Coalicion de Creadeores, a pressure group of copyright holders.

Since 2013, a new law has been in development, commonly known as "Ley Lassale". It does not represent a new law as such, but rather a modification and update of the "Ley Sinde". The most controversial element of this new version is the possibility of advertisers on websites found to be hosting content that infringes copyright being fined from 30,000 to 600,000 euros. From the users' perspective, the big innovation within the new law is the recognition of legal private copies when made directly from an original.

Legal and Regulatory Basis of Approach

The *Ley Sinde* in 2009 created the Comission de Propriedad Intelectual as the primary vehicle by which the Spanish state tackles online copyright infringe. The commission has two sections (i) consisting of three members named by the minister of education, culture and sports which is responsible for mediation and settling claims; (ii) formed by the secretary of culture and four representatives from the ministry of culture, economy, industry and the presidency office. The first section, "*Seccion primera*" is a regulatory body which defines the policy on copyright issues and possible tariffs to be applied, the rules on private copies – it has an almost legislative capacity (through it's still unclear). The second commission, "*Seccion segunda*", works in practice as a fast paced court for copyright issues with the whole decision making process taking less than 15 days. Judges and normal courts are only involved for rectifying decisions that do not address copyright, just fundamental rights like freedom of speech.

Enforcement Process

The owner of the protected material can raise a complaint with the "Comission de Propriedad Intelectual", which has mediation and arbitration powers in copyright infringement issues. If the infringing party is not identified, the Commission has the power to request (through the judicial system) for the ISPs to take down the identified websites and provide information that might lead to the identification of the infringing party. If the court (Audiencia Nacional) allows for the requested information to be shared (which must happen during a 24 hour period) then the Commission might issue compensation up to 300,000 euros.

After a decision from the Commission for removal of content, the ISP has 48 hours to decide how to proceed. If it takes down the material the procedure is over, alternatively it might present evidence and arguments against the decision. This process can last up to seven days, and the Commission should make a new decision in the following three days. This means that the process might last approximately 15 days. But the implementation of its resolution can only be carried out after publishing a decision from the Central Court of Administrative litigation. This effectively means that the case will have to bounce back to the judicial system. However this is still an improvement over the previous proposal where a claimant did not have to offer any proof that there had been damage, just that the offending site was "likely to cause property damage", so it significantly increases the burden of proof.

The legal framework has been heavily criticized as most of the decisions can be made without the interference of a judge[128]. This clearly constitutes a problem in a situation where copyright holders may have a greater influence over the deciding bodies. Also, and commonly referred to by the consumer groups, the cases discussed in the Commission are not brought by anyone within the judicial system or the authorities, but by complaints made by copyright holders. This gives copyright holders some arbitrary powers where they do not necessarily target websites that actually profit by causing damage (like illegal commercially oriented torrent sites) as they might be hard to identify or litigate. A common concern is that copyright holders might opt instead to identify and target individual users regardless of their level of activity.

Enforcement Measures / Sanctions

The Commission can sanction sites that infringe copyright to pay up to 300,000 euros in compensation. Advertisers that place adverts with sites that host illegal content can also be sanctioned up to 600,000 euros.

"Ley Lassale" also introduces an innovation that is presently under discussion. It is colloquially known as the "google tax" as it proposes to charge some content providers (like *Google news*, and *Yahoo news*) for the use of publicly available information of content producers like newspapers or magazines. The proposed mechanism for this would not be a direct payment to the owner of the content but to a representative Collective Management Organisation (CMO) that would create a fund. However details about the fund structure, management and goals are still unclear.

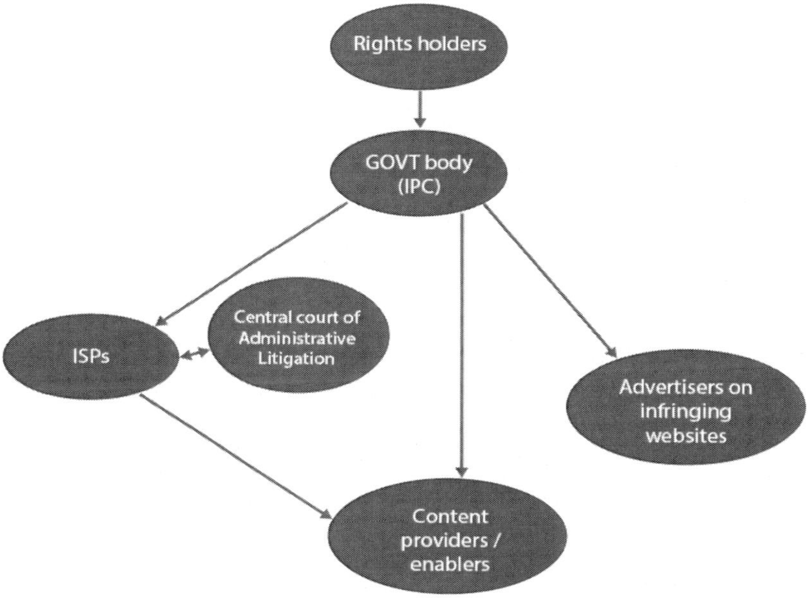

Source: BOP Consulting with DotEcon (2014).

Figure 15. Institutional configuration of the enforcement process in Spain.

Burden and Standard of Proof

The standard of proof is a common criticism of the current legislative framework. Decisions are made by the "Commission de Propriedad Intelectual" that is not part of the judicial system. Decisions are only rectified by a judge, not based on the evidence presented but only to confirm that the decision made respects fundamental rights (i.e. Freedom of speech).

Costs

The *Comission de Propriedad Intelectual* is not an autonomous body and it runs under the influence of three different ministries; a separate budget for the Commission is not available For the complaints raised to the "commission segunda" the costs are by default imputed to the rights holder party, or shared if agreed in advance. The Commission has the power to assign any additional costs (i.e. research) to both parties on a pro-rata basis as defined in Article 5 of the legislation. As the decisions made by the Commission are not made in a court, they have the potential to be later overturned in a court. If this happens, damage has been made to the host of the material under dispute. The law contemplates a compensation, to be defined by the judge, for these situations. In which case, the compensation will be paid directly by the Commission. This institutional arrangement suggests a scenario in which cases may become decided not only or even mainly on merit, but on the degree of financial risk that they may expose the Commission to (and ergo the government).

Implementation, Monitoring and Effectiveness

The approach has been in operation for just over 2.5 years. Since instigation, no defined reporting mechanism has been put in place regarding how the measures are monitored or assessed for their effectiveness. On a sporadic basis, the Ministry of Culture has reported on the number of complaints raised and the total number of cases completed. For 2013, for instance the following statistics have been published:

- 363 requests were received by the IPC;
- 248 were archived as they were deemed to be incomplete;
- 115 requests were accepted;
- 30 requests were under analysis;
- 4 requests were suspended as the material was removed by the infringing party during the process; and
- 81 requests were being researched.

The lack of any further usable statistics means that it is not possible to make any real assessment of the effectiveness of the approach.

UNITED KINGDOM

Overview of the UK Approach

The UK approach focuses on both individual subscribers engaging in infringing activities and those providing infringing material and enabling access to such material:

1) Individual users accessing infringing material will be targeted through a voluntary scheme agreed between the British Phonographic Industry ("BPI"), the Motion Picture Association ("MPA") and the four largest Internet Service Providers ("ISPs") - BT, Sky, TalkTalk and Virgin Media). Under the scheme, copyright owners will identify individuals engaging in unlawful peer-to-peer ("P2P") file sharing and inform the ISP who will send a notification of alleged infringement to the account holder. The purpose of this scheme is mainly educational, and it will be supported by an educational campaign that will receive significant funding from the UK Government. The scheme - known as Creative Content UK – will be implemented in 2015 beginning with the multi-media educational campaign, followed shortly after by the sending of notices; and
2) Action against the enablers of infringement such as those websites providing access to infringing material can be taken under UK copyright law (the Copyright, Designs and Patents Act, CDPA). Under the CDPA website owners found by the courts to be infringing copyright can be fined and or imprisoned. Legislation provides for a notice and action regime where the rights holder identifies infringing material and takes steps to take down the content or to request ISPs to block access to that content. Sections 18 and 19 of the Electronic Commerce (EC Directive) Regulations 2002 provide an incentive for ISPs to remove infringing material or block access to material hosted in the UK if they have been notified by the rights holder of the existence of such material. Doing so 'expeditiously' means that they escape any liability for copyright infringement to which they might otherwise be exposed. Section 97A of the Copyright, Designs and Patent Act 1988 ("CDPA") entitles rights holders to seek court injunctions against ISPs that require the blocking of subscriber access to infringing material. This is of particular importance where that material is hosted outside of the UK are more difficult to target via notice and takedown requests.

There is complementary support from the police in the form of a dedicated, operationally independent enforcement unit – the Police Intellectual Property Crime Unit (PIPCU). PIPCU funded by the IPO (£2.56m funding for two years) was established in September 2013 with a remit to tackle serious and organised intellectual property crime with a focus on offences committed online. One of PIPCU's major operations has been 'Operation Creative' which aims to disrupt and prevent online copyright infringing websites by engaging with site owners, disrupting advertising revenue and de-registering domain names.[129]

Contextual Factors

The UK has well-developed residential broadband and an increasing number of legal online services for streaming and downloading digital content or subscription services with a particular focus on music, TV and movies.

Ofcom's latest research into broadband speeds (conducted in May 2014) showed that in the UK, the average actual speed for residential fixed-line broadband connections was 18.7Mbit/s. Furthermore, standard broadband coverage in the UK is around 95-100% and 'superfast' broadband[130] coverage is approximately 70-75%.[131] For the UK, Fixed Broadband penetration is reported as 35.73/100 – 4th out of the 9 countries covered in this report for the IPO.[132]

In the UK, consumers have access to all major legal services[133] and there are a growing number of alternative legal services. For example, the Pro-Music data – which is compiled by the IFPI[134] and based on information supplied by its local industry groups – shows that, at the time of writing, there were 62 legal online music services available in the UK,[135] more than any other country in our study according to the Pro-Music data.

Furthermore, customer research conducted by Kantar Media[136] (Copyright Infringement Tracker, Wave 4, September 2013[137] covering the three month period from March to May 2013) it was shown that awareness of legal alternatives had grown since Wave 3 and over each of the first four reviews. In particular, for TV and movies, "*[a]wareness of Netflix (64%), Google Play (33%) and Blinkbox (25%) saw significant rises compared to the previous quarter*" a trend that was also see between Wave 3 (covering the period November 2012 to January 2013) and Wave 2 (covering the period of August to October 2012) of the study. Similarly for music services, awareness of Spotify (44%), Last FM (17%) and Steam (12%) also saw small but significant rises in awareness since previous waves.[138]

Whilst awareness of legal services is increasing, the price of legal content online appears to be a significant factor for individuals consuming infringing content with 49% of consumers citing "because it is free" as their primary reason for infringing, and 32% saying that a greater availability of cheaper legal services would encourage them to stop infringing.[139] More work also needs to be done to educate customers as to which online resources are legal and which are infringing with 34% of consumers asking for greater clarity about what is legal and what is not (24%). These findings show that greater education, supporting new and existing legal alternatives and pointing users in the direction of these could potentially be successful in reducing the level of copyright infringement. The Creative Content UK scheme discussed below should help in this regard.

Background and Policy Process

Whilst the CDPA has been in place since 1988, online copyright infringement is a relatively recent phenomenon that has been the subject of a number of independent reviews and consultations. In July 2006, the Gowers Review of the UK intellectual property framework identified unlawful P2P file sharing as a major threat to the creative industries and called for action to be taken to combat online copyright infringement. Prompted by the findings of the Gowers Review, in summer 2008 the Government encouraged several ISPs and rights holders to sign a Memorandum of Understanding under which industry players would work together to improve awareness of the illegal nature of P2P file sharing among consumers.

At the same time a consultation was published setting out proposals to bring other ISPs into the regime and to impose specific duties on Ofcom to address the issue of online copyright infringement. Following the consultation, the Department for Culture, Media and Sport and the Department for Business, Innovation and Skills published 'Digital Britain: The Interim Report' in January 2009 outlining the need for further legislation. The proposed legislation would require ISPs to notify infringers that their conduct is unlawful and to collect information on serious repeat infringers that should be made available to rights-holders on an anonymised basis. Rights holders could seek a court order to obtain personal details which would then allow them to bring legal action against infringers. The initial findings and proposals were developed in 'Digital Britain: Final Report', a Government White Paper published in June 2009. This then led to the Digital Economy Bill, which was introduced to Parliament in November 2009 and received Royal Assent in April 2010 thereby becoming the Digital Economy Act 2010 ("DEA").

The DEA formally set out the provisions for the proposed notifications scheme. Under an initial obligations code to be developed by OFCOM, ISPs would be required to notify subscribers of alleged infringement and to take measures that make it easier for rights holders to bring legal action against repeat infringers. If those initial obligations were found to be ineffective, the DEA also included the option for further obligations to be imposed on ISPs under which they would have to adopt technical measures (such as degrading connections or cutting off subscribers) to combat infringement.

The Impact Assessments published alongside the DEA estimated that, absent intervention, the costs to copyright owners (including TV, cinema, music, entertainment software and video games) in terms of displaced sales due to illegal file sharing would be in the region of £400 million per annum. Balancing the estimated costs of implementing the regime against the benefits to rights holders from recovering displaced sales, it was considered that the net benefit (assessed in NPV terms calculated over a ten year period) could be as high as £1.2billion.

Legal and Regulatory Basis of Approach

The legal basis for proceeding against providers of infringing material is given by the CDPA. Under section 2A of the CDPA deliberate infringement of copyright (piracy) by communicating the work to the public is a criminal offence with criminal liability: "a) in the course of a business, or b) otherwise than in the course of a business to such an extent as to affect prejudicially the owner of the copyright" if the person knows or has reason to believe that, by doing so, he/she is infringing copyright in that work. This is not specific to but includes online infringement of copyright.

These provisions work in conjunction with the Electronic Commerce (EC Directive) Regulations 2002, transposing into UK law the European Commission E-Commerce Directive (Directive 2000/31/EC), which stipulate that a caching or hosting service provider is not liable for copyright infringement on its service provided that, upon becoming aware of the infringing material, the service provider acts expeditiously to remove such material or block access to it. This should provide incentives for ISPs to respond to requests from rights holders to remove or block access to infringing material as they might otherwise be liable for copyright infringement, but can escape such liability by acting upon such requests.[140]

Rights holders can seek an injunction requiring ISPs to block access to infringing material hosted outside UK jurisdiction under Section 97A of the CDPA. This section was introduced into the CDPA by the Copyright and

Related Rights Regulations 2003, which transposed the EC Copyright Directive.[141]

Looking at users who are accessing illegal content, the DEA would provide the legal basis for enforcement. However, the DEA provisions have not yet been implemented and the initial obligations code has not been finalised. Following the delays in the implementation of the DEA, a Copyright Alerts Programme ("CAP") has been established between BPI, MPA and the four major ISPs. The CAP involves a similar style notification scheme, which will come into force in 2015, but will be largely educational in nature and will not result in punitive measures. The CAP is one part of Creative Content UK, a partnership between content creators and ISPs with support from government. Together with the CAP there will be a major educational awareness campaign about the value of online content, legal source and to help reduce online copyright infringement.

Enforcement Process

Enforcement relies on rights holders identifying infringement in the first instance. A rights holder becoming aware of infringing content online, such as a website providing access to infringing material or used primarily to facilitate copyright infringement has several options:

- notifying the website operator, hosting provider or domain registrar in the relevant territory that there is a high level of infringing content on a particular website and requesting that the content be removed (cease and desist request);
- sending a notice and takedown request to the relevant ISP, which should action valid and genuine notice and takedown requests using the provision under the E-commerce directive; typically this will be used for websites and content hosted in the UK;
- where approaches to the website owner, or hosting provider are unsuccessful, applying to the High Court for an injunction under section 97A of the CDPA to order an ISP to take action, e.g. block subscriber access to the infringing website; this is typically used against infringing content hosted outside the UK. In practice, ISPs were initially concerned about blocking access to websites in their entirety due to the lack of legal certainty. However, given the increasing number of court orders requiring ISPs to block access,

there is case precedent in this area, and the process has been streamlined; and

- involving PIPCU where evidence is provided to show criminal infringement. Rights holders will notify PIPCU of the infringing website together with evidence indicating how the site is involved in illegal copyright infringement. PIPCU will check and verify whether the website is infringing and if confirmed, will notify the site owner of the illegal activity and request co-operation with the police to address this. If the site owner fails to engage with the police the website is added to an Infringing Website List ("IWL") shared with major brands and advertising agencies with a request to cease advertising on that site (an attempt to drain revenue streams to the infringing site). Persistent offenders will be targeted by the sending of formal letters to domain name registrars from PIPCU requesting that the domain name is suspended until further notice as the website is facilitating criminal copyright infringement under UK law.

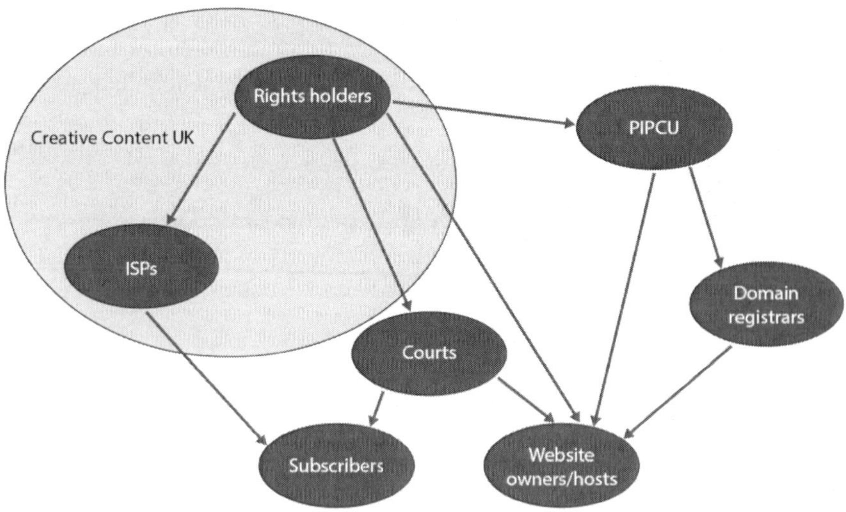

Source: BOP Consulting with DotEcon (2014).

Figure 16. Institutional configuration of the enforcement process in the UK.

Once operational, under the Creative Content UK notification scheme, rights holders will also be able to identify infringing activity undertaken by an individual partaking in P2P file sharing and send a notification to the ISP. In this case, the rights holder should provide evidence, including the IP address, to the relevant ISP. The ISP will then be obliged to pass on the notification of alleged infringement to the owner of the account to warn them that illegal behaviour has taken place on their account and inform them of legal alternatives.

Enforcement Measures / Sanctions

Individuals do not face sanctions under the voluntary regime. The notification scheme is purely educational.

Infringing websites owners can face fines and or imprisonment. A person guilty of an offence under subsection 2A of the CDPA is liable:

- on summary conviction to imprisonment for a term not exceeding three months or a fine not exceeding £50,000, or both; and
- on conviction on indictment to a fine or imprisonment for a term not exceeding two years, or both.[142]

In addition, PIPCU attempts to disrupt advertising revenue to sites listed on the IWL. As part of 'Project Sunblock' PIPCU has been replacing advertising on copyright infringing websites with "official force banners" that warn users that the site is illegal / under criminal investigation and advise them to exit the website.[143]

Burden and Standard of Proof

Exact details of the burden and standard of proof that rights holders have to meet in order to identify infringing behaviour of individuals and subsequently notify ISPs are not available. Some guidance may be taken from the proposals made in relation to the implementation of the DEA, but there may be variations in the approach eventually used.

Under the notice and action process when determining whether a hosting service provider "has actual knowledge" of infringing material, a court may consider whether the service provider has received a notice and whether the notice included, inter alia, sufficient detail of the location of the information in question and the details of the unlawful nature of the activity or information in question. ISPs stress the importance of having legal certainty before they take action against infringers/infringing content.

In general, a balance needs to be struck between ensuring that there is not a prohibitive burden on rights holders, yet ISPs are sufficiently confident that the evidence provided is sufficient to take action.

Costs

While there have been few measures of the total costs of implementation, we are aware of the funding provided by the government to support the implementation of a number of the policy measures discussed above, and there were some estimates of the costs of sending notifications put forward in the context of the impact assessment of the DEA proposals.

IPO funding of PIPCU amounts to £2.56m for the first 2 years. The government will provide funding of the educational campaign for Creative Content UK of £3.5m over 3 years, and industry funding will amount to £0.5m.

At the time of the DEA the impact assessment of notification scheme (from DEA) considered the costs to ISPs of complying with legislation to be in the region of £290-500 million in total.[144] Whilst these may provide some indication of the costs faced by ISPs in implementing the scheme, the exact costs under the voluntary regime will differ to the extent that the process requirements may not be as strict as proposed under the DEA.

The DEA impact assessment report also presents some estimates provided to it of the cost to copyright owners of detecting infringements and generating copyright infringement reports ("CIRs"): 2 million CIRs cost £0.8 million; 4 million CIRs costs £1.6 million and; 6 million CIRs cost £2.8 million. This would suggest increasing marginal costs and amount to between £0.4 - £0.47 per CIR.[145]

More recent costs of processing CIRs for five major fixed line ISPs in the UK, were estimated in a report by BCWS Ltd. published alongside Ofcom's Consultation on the cost sharing order. A provisional estimate suggested that at 100,000 copyright infringement reports per ISP per month, the cost of processing each CIR would amount to £2.93.[146]

Taking the combined cost and assuming that each of the five major fixed line ISPs would process around 100,000 reports per month for the first two years, the total cost would be around £40 million.

Implementation, Monitoring and Effectiveness

The first UK High Court Order for blocking was in 2011 (Newzbin2 case[147])– since then around 10 more court orders have resulted in the blocking of around 40 websites. The IP Crime Group's 2013 report stated in relation to site blocking that the "civil action taken by copyright owner has had the knock on effect where a number of international infringing sites have voluntary sought not to be accessible from the UK."[148] The IP Crime Group also reports annually on the number of files, links and websites successfully taken down by right holders.[149] However, it does not monitor its effectiveness in terms of the impact on levels of copyright infringement.

PIPCU became operational in September 2013. The IWL was introduced after PIPCU ran a three month pilot scheme. According to PIPCU the "pilot saw a clear and positive trend, with a 12% reduction in advertising from major household brands on the identified illegal websites."[150] However, further information on the effectiveness of the scheme has not been published since it has been launched. As well as the IWL PIPCU has been contacting domain registrars of persistent infringing websites, asking the registrar to suspend the domain. In May 2014, several major copyright infringing website had closed down as a result of PIPCU's initiative[151] and has resulted in 2.5 million visits to copyright infringing sites being diverted to a domain suspension page.[152] However, it is not evident what effect this has had on infringement levels and or traffic to websites that provide legitimate access to music, films and books that are signposted on PIPCU's domain suspension page.

Creative Content UK is due to come into force in 2015. Nothing has been formalised for monitoring the effectiveness of the schemes coming into force as a result of the Creative Content UK. However, given significant government funding, it is expected that there will need to be some level of monitoring of its impact.

THE UNITED STATES

Overview of the US Approach

The US approach works predominantly by providing a safe harbour to online service providers that protects them from being liable for copyright infringement provided that:

1) they take measures to remove any infringing material or access to such material as soon as they become aware that this material is available on its network. Service providers may become aware of the infringing content and activity through their own initiative, but most likely will be notified of claimed infringement by copyright owners (or representatives of copyright owners) via a 'notification of infringement'. At this point they must remove or disable access to the material (i.e. there is a 'notice and takedown' regime to target access to infringing material); and
2) they adopt and implement a policy that allows for the termination of access to their network for repeat infringers and notifies subscribers of this; and co-operate with subpoenas where a copyright owner wants to identify an alleged infringer. A voluntary scheme – the Copyright Alert System (CAS) – was set up to allow service providers to notifying individual infringers that their behaviour is illegal and notify repeat infringers of the consequences under the safe harbour conditions.[153] Although the emphasis of the scheme is on education, punitive measures may apply for repeat infringers and ISPs must keep a record so that they can provide this information to copyright owners if they receive a subpoena or court order.

Legal action can be taken against copyright infringers with rights holders claiming actual damages and profits. Alternatively, rights holders can claim statutory damages.

Contextual Factors

Residential broadband in the US is relatively well developed and there has been a significant increase in the provision of legal services for digital movies, music and TV shows over the past five years. However, as in the UK, there is still a role for educational campaigns to improve consumer awareness and clarity between what is legal and what is illegal.

The Federal Communications Commission's ("FCC") latest annual "Measuring Broadband America" report, published in April 2014 [154] (taking September 2013 as its reference month) found an average subscribed speed of 21.2 Mbps, representing an increase of about 36% from the 15.6 Mbps average the previous year.[155]

The report also found that ISPs provide 101% of advertised speeds meaning that consumers are receiving a connection that delivers on the subscribed speed. For the US, Fixed Broadband penetration is reported as 28.54/100 – 6th out of the 9 countries covered in this report for the IPO.[156]

In the US, consumers have access to all major legal services[157] and there are a growing number of alternative legal services. In its one-year review of the CAS, the Center for Copyright Information (CCI) acknowledged the increase in legal sources for digital movies, music and TV shows over the past five years and refers to easily accessible and affordable legal services like Spotify, Beats Music, Hulu and Netflix.[158] Furthermore, the industry-sourced data from Pro-music, compiled by the IFPI,[159] shows that there were 56 legal online music services available in the US at the time of writing.[160]

The CCI claims that its recent research into attitudes about P2P use and copyright infringement shows that *"the present availability of large amounts of authorized entertainment content online has led to an increase in the number of people who report accessing content from authorized sources"*.[161] The CCI found that 50% of those surveyed reported to have accessed movies or TV shows using online legitimate services and more than 70% reported to have used these services for music.[162]

In its one-year review of the CAS, the CCI presented research undertaken by Screen Digest, showing that by 2013, the number of movies viewed, rented or purchased through legal methods (including ad-supported and subscription streaming) had increased by fifteen times the levels seen in 2009 and was up to 5.7 billion movies. Similarly, equivalent figures for TV shows were up 175%, over the same period to 56 billion TV shows.[163] The CCI also refers to data from the RIAA showing that, over the same period 5 year period, subscribers to paid on-demand music services grew over 400%.[164]

However, in line with the findings of Kantar Media in the UK, there is still some work to do to improve the clarity between what is legal and what is illegal, as the CCI found that 65% of the respondents to consumer research conducted in February 2014, agreed that *"more resources need to made available that make clear which sources and activities are/are not legal."* 165 Therefore, the educational aspect of the CCI's schemes is clearly important and this is discussed in more detail below.

Background and Policy Process

The underlying legislation for enforcement of copyright online is the 1998 Digital Millennium Copyright Act ("DMCA"), signed into law in October 28 1998.

One of the primary functions of the DMCA is to transpose two 1996 World Intellectual Property Organisation (WIPO) treaties into US national law. Title 1 of the DMCA implements the WIPO Copyright Treaty and the WIPO Performances and Phonograms Treaty. The main changes required by these treaties were to recognise copyrights of work from other countries and to make foreign works exempt from a rule requiring copyright owners to register their work with the US Copyright Office before they can raise a lawsuit regarding infringement of their work. The amendments also made it illegal to circumvent technological measures taken to prevent people from accessing or copying a work to which they do not have a legal right (except where people make a copy of a work for fair use). [166]

However, the DMCA also included provisions to update US copyright law to deal with online copyright infringement, and Title 2 of the DMCA is the most relevant in this regard. It introduces the Online Copyright Infringement Liability Limitation Act ("OCILLA"), which grants copyright liability limitation for online service providers[167] on the condition that they have certain policies and procedures in place.

Legal and Regulatory Basis of Approach

The legal basis of the notice and takedown is the 1998 Digital Millennium Copyright Act ("DMCA"), with particular emphasis on the Online Copyright Infringement Liability Limitation Act ("OCILLA").

Specifically, a service provider is protected from liability for infringement taking place on their network or for allowing access to websites containing infringing material unknowingly provided it takes measures to remove any infringing material or access to such material as soon as it becomes aware that this material is available on its network,[168] adopts and implements a policy that allows for the termination of access to its network for repeat infringers and notifies their subscribers of this;[169] and co-operates with subpoenas where a copyright owner wants to identify an alleged infringer thus facilitating the copyright owner to take legal action.[170]

In addition to the DMCA, a group of artists, content creators and service providers has formed a consortium called the 'Center for Copyright Information' ("CCI"). Members of the CCI include the Recording Industry Association of America (RIAA), Motion Picture Association of America (MPAA), AT&T, Cablevision, Comcast, Time Warner Cable, and Verizon.[171] Together they have established a scheme known as the Copyright Alert System ("CAS"), which was designed to "educate consumers about the importance of copyright protection and to offer information about online copyright infringement".[172] At the same time, this scheme allows the service providers to fulfil the second safe harbour condition.

The CAS is a voluntary agreement. All participating members have signed a formal Memorandum of Understanding ("MOU"), which provides details about the CAS and outlines the roles and procedures participating members must follow. In addition to the industry players, the CCI has an 'Advisory Board' which can provide guidance and consult on any issues associated with the scheme, such as the design and implementation of education schemes and the CAS.

Enforcement Process

The rights holder (or its representative) will typically identify infringing material and notify the online service provider (elements of such a notification are outlined in Section 202 of the DMCA inserting §513(c)(3) into the United States Code) i.e. the scheme is reactive. Upon receiving such information, the service provider must act "expeditiously to remove, or disable access to the material".[173]

To reduce the impact of false positives (i.e. removal of non-infringing material) the DMCA allows for counter notifications to be made. Elements of such a notification are outlined in Section 202 of the DMCA inserting §512(g)(3) into the United States Code. Following receipt of a counter notification – provided there is sufficient evidence to show that the removal was a result of mistake or misidentification – the material must be reinstated, or blocking ceased in between 10-14 business days following receipt of the counter notification.

Under the CAS, copyright owners identify infringing content on P2P networks and collect evidence on the IP address of the suspected infringer and provide these details to the ISP together with details of date, time and time zone of the alleged P2P online infringement. The ISP then sends notification letters to that subscriber including educational information regarding copyright law and legal sources. A subscriber may receive up to six notification letters, each increasing in the strength of its content. After multiple letters ISPs have the discretion to temporarily affect that subscriber's Internet connection. ISPs must keep a record of repeat infringers and copyright owners can issue a subpoena to obtain details of these infringers.

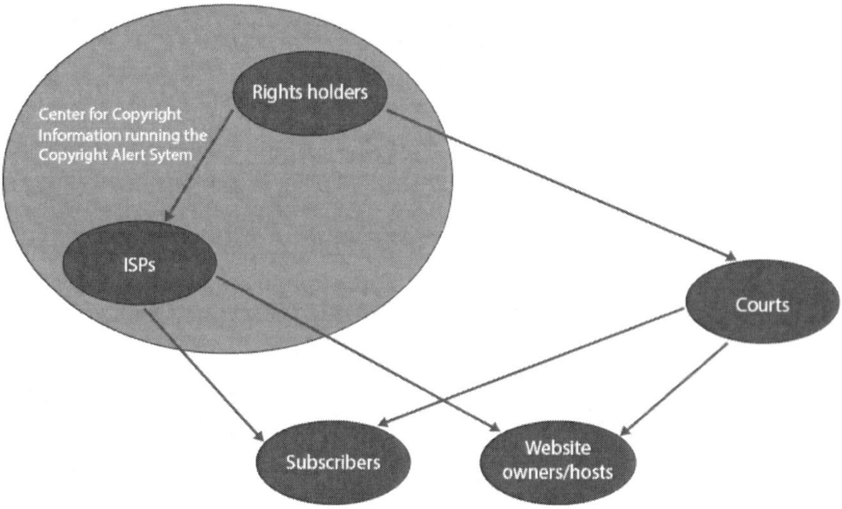

Source: BOP Consulting with DotEcon (2014).

Figure 17. Institutional configuration of the enforcement process in the US.

Enforcement Measures / Sanctions

The OCILLA protects service providers from legal action they may otherwise face if infringing behaviour were to take place on their network, or for allowing access to websites containing infringing material.[174]

Legal action can be taken against copyright infringers with rights holders claiming actual damages and a restitution of profits made from infringements.[175] Alternatively, rights holders can claim statutory damages.[176]

Rights holders can claim statutory damages for general copyright infringement with respect to any one work, for which any one infringer is liable individually, or for which any two or more infringers are liable jointly and severally, in a sum of not less than $750 or more than $30,000 as the court considers just. The court has the discretion to increase this amount to $150,000 for wilful infringement, and reduce it to no less than $200 if the infringement occurred without the infringer being aware.[177]

The CAS is primarily educational in that at least the first five notifications sent to an individual are educational and/or warnings. It is only after the individual receives at least five notifications that a 'mitigation measure copyright alert' is sent. Following the issue of a 'mitigation measure copyright alert' ISPs have the discretion to temporarily affect that subscriber's Internet connection through means such as:

a) temporary reduction in uploading and/or downloading transmission speeds;
b) temporary step-down in the Subscriber's service tier to (1) the lowest tier of Internet access service above dial-up service that the Participating ISP makes widely available to residential customers in the Subscriber's community, or (2) an alternative bandwidth throughput rate low enough to significantly impact a Subscriber's broadband Internet access service (e.g., 256 - 640 kbps);
c) temporary redirection to a Landing Page until the Subscriber contacts the Participating ISP to discuss with it the Copyright Alerts;
d) temporary restriction of the Subscriber's Internet access for some reasonable period of time as determined in the Participating ISP's discretion;
e) temporary redirection to a Landing Page for completion of a meaningful educational instruction on copyright; or
f) such other temporary Mitigation Measure as may be applied by the Participating ISP in its discretion that is designed to be comparable to those Mitigation Measures described above."[178]

Burden and Standard of Proof

For infringement notifications under the DMCA, rights owners are required to provide information to a designated agent of the service provider in line with the requirements set out in the DMCA which includes, amongst other details, to clearly identify the work that has been infringed, information reasonably sufficient to permit the service provider to locate the material and a statement that the information in the notification is accurate, and under penalty of perjury, that the complaining party is authorized to act on behalf of the owner of an exclusive right that is allegedly infringed.[179]

If the notification fails to comply with these requirements, then it will be deemed to be insufficient to prove that a service provider had "actual knowledge or is aware of facts or circumstances from which infringing activity is apparent" and therefore may not result in takedown or blocking of access to the infringing material.

Under the CAS, the copyright owners are required to develop and maintain written methodologies for the identification of online copyright infringement using P2P technology that comply with the requirements set out in the MOU.[180] These methodologies are reviewed periodically by an independent and impartial technical expert or experts retained by the CCI and rights holders must not send infringement notifications before the methodology has been reviewed and evaluated by the Independent expert and it has not been issued a Finding of Inadequacy.[181]

Subscribers who have received a mitigation alert have fourteen days to file a request for an independent review by the American Arbitration Association (AAA) and can challenge the copyright alerts on the following grounds: misidentification of account; unauthorized use of account; authorized use of copyright material; fair use under prevailing principles of copyright law; misidentification of file; and if the work in question was published before 1923.[182]

In relation to the setting of statutory damages, copyright owners sustain the burden of proving that an infringement was committed wilfully, and the infringer bears the burden of proof in relation to showing that was not aware or, and had no reason to believe, that it was infringing copyright.

Costs

We are not aware of any evidence or analysis of the costs of implementing the CAS, or the costs incurred by rights holders and ISPs in identifying infringing content and removing or blocking access to infringing material respectively under the 'notice and action' regime.

For the CAS, half of the funding for the CCI will be provided by the Participating Content Owners Group, with the other half coming from the Participating ISPs.[183] The MOU does not specify whether the costs of identifying alleged infringers, or the costs of sending notifications are included in the costs incurred by the CCI and therefore also split equally between content owners and ISPs.

Implementation, Monitoring and Effectiveness

Whilst the DMCA was passed in 1998, the CAS came into operation only in February 2013.[184]

There do not appear to be any requirements for regular assessment of the effectiveness of the 'notice and takedown' procedure.

One of the obligations of the CCI is to provide annual reports assessing the effectiveness of the copyright enforcement (although this focuses heavily on the CAS). The assessment is made based on the evidence provided by copyright owners and the ISPs in their semi-annual reports.

Much of the initial assessment appears to be based on measures such as the number of notifications at various levels rather than an assessment of the impacts the notifications are having on the level of infringement or on use of legitimate online services. Indeed, in its first annual review of the scheme the CCI concentrated its analysis on the number of notifications at the different stages, but noting that "a very small fraction" of the number of accounts receiving alerts during the analysis period were Mitigation alerts (8%), "with less than 3% at the final (or second) Mitigation level."[185]

End Notes

[1] For this reason, the South Korean government is reviewing the current institutional arrangements and consolidating them into a new Copyright Protection Board.

[2] The UK had a comprehensive monitoring scheme in place in the form of quarterly surveys, but only four reports were issued before the funding, and subsequently the reporting, ceased. However, the four waves of the Kantar Media survey commissioned by Ofcom and the IPO that were undertaken will be used as a baseline against which future trends can be benchmarked.

[3] N.B. While the number of fixed line broadband accounts seem far lower than wireless accounts in Figure 1, this is because fixed line accounts are shared among all members of a household whereas mobile accounts only serve individual subscribers.

[4] See, for instance, the review of UK industry-based surveys of consumers, looking at both online and offline infringement, contained in BOP (2010) *Changing Attitudes and Behaviour in the 'non-internet' digital world and their implications for Intellectual Property*, report for the Strategic Advisory Board on Intellectual Property.

[5] IFPI (2014) *Digital Music Report 2014*.

[6] The data comes from the second wave of the 2013 time series representative survey that is used to develop a 'barometer' of the legal offer in France. It is undertaken by Harris Interactive and commissioned by *HADOPI* and reported on in the *HADOPI Annual Report 2014*. The highest consumer satisfaction of the legal offer is reserved instead for photos, games and software, which all have over 70%+ satisfaction in France.

[7] See HADOPI (*ibid*). The first wave of the Harris Interactive survey was carried out in January 2013 and the second wave undertaken in September 2013.

[8] Spotify for instance has published their own 'Spotify's impact on piracy' research, which reviews a small number of country studies that suggests that legal streaming services are turning the tide against piracy, with previously illegal users migrating to legal consumption (Spotify, 2013, https://www.spotifyartists.com/spotifyexplained/#spotifys-impact-on-piracy). Other studies that look at the levels of traffic to individual legal services compared with traffic to sites known to contain very high levels of copyright infringing content, suggest similar conclusions. For instance, a 2012 Sandvine report covering North America reported that Netflix represented 24.4% of total internet traffic volume in North America over one 24 hour period, well ahead of BitTorrent, at 14.2% (https://www.sandvine.com).

[9] The statistic comes from the fourth wave of Kantar Media's survey – Kantar Media (2013) *Online Copyright Infringement Tracker: Wave 4 – Overview and key findings.*

[10] The quote comes from an Address by the Director General to the WIPO Assemblies 2013. Available online at: http://www.wipo.int/about-wipo/en/dgo/speeches/a 51 dg speech.html

[11] For instance, in the last wave of Kantar Media's 2013 UK-based survey, 34% of consumers asked for greater clarity about what is legal and a further 24% asked for more clarity about what is not. Similarly in a 2012 Dutch survey (Leenheer and Poort, 2014 – see Dutch case study below), while one third of the population is 'well aware' of the current laws and regulations concerning content from an illegal source, one third of the population is 'not aware' of laws and regulations and the remaining third is only 'more or less aware'.

[12] de Dios Montoro Pons, J. and Cuadrado Garcia, M. (2008) 'Legal origin and intellectual property rights: an empirical study in the pre-recorded music sector', in *European Journal of Law and Economics*, 26:153–173

[13] In particular, the study first tries to group the different countries under five distinct legal systems. However, this does not produce conclusive results. After this analysis, the authors then group all of the countries into just two groups, common and civil law. While the common law group of countries are a coherent group (Australia, Canada, Ireland, New Zealand, UK, USA) the 'civil law' grouping brings together systems that are not homogenous. It would therefore have been more honest to call the two groups: common law and 'not common law'. Further, a factor that the authors do not control for is that all the common law countries are English speaking, so any effect that the research might be picking up in the 'common law' group may actually be something to do with English language (e.g. that this kind of content was widely available through legal channels during the period but non-English language content was less widely available) rather than the common law legal system.

[14] South Korea is an exception in this case as their graduated response system has actually resulted in a large number of convictions.

[15] See https://www.ic.gc.ca/eic/site/crp-prda.nsf/eng/h_rp01153.html

[16] See Table 5.3.10 of "Communications Monitoring Report 2014: Telecommunications Sector"; Canadian Radio-television and Telecommunications Commission. Available at: http://www.crtc.gc.ca/eng/publications/reports/ PolicyMonitoring/2014/cmr5.htm

[17] http://news.gc.ca/web/article-en.do?nid=899999

[18] Figures are based on end 2013 data for fixed (wired)-broadband subscriptions as published in the "18th edition of the World Telecommunication/ICT Indicators Database"; International Telecommunication Union, 2014. Available at: http://www.itu.int/en/ITU-D/Statistics/Pages/stat/default.aspx.

[19] Including, Netflix, Itunes (music, movies, TV shows), Youtube, Google Play (Movies, TV Shows, music), Spotify.

[20] Including, Netflix, Itunes (music, movies, TV shows), Youtube, Google Play (Movies, TV Shows, music), Spotify.

[21] http://www.ifpi.org/about.php

[22] Including: 7digital, Archambault, ArtistXite, Bell, CBC Music, Classical Archives, Daily Motion, Deezer, eMusic, Google Play, HMV Digital, iTunes, Mediazoic, Mixradio, Motime, MTV, Music Unlimited, Naxos, Qello, rara.com, Rdio, Slacker, Songza, Spotify, Stingray Music, Vevo, Xbox Music, YouTube, Zik.

[23] See page 104 of International Intellectual Property Alliance (Iipa) 2014 Special 301 Report On Copyright Protection And Enforcement. Available at http://www.iipa.com/rbc/2014 /2014SPEC301CANADA.PDF

[24] See page 104 of International Intellectual Property Alliance (Iipa) 2014 Special 301 Report On Copyright Protection And Enforcement. Available at http://www.iipa.com/rbc/2014 /2014SPEC301CANADA.PDF

[25] See Industry Canada, Digital Canada 150: http://www.ic.gc.ca/eic/site /028.nsf/eng /home#item22

[26] Provisions for the notification regime are contained in sections 41.25 and 41.26 of the Copyright Modernization Act. Section 35 of the Copyright Modernization Act clarifies that ISPs, hosts and search engines are not liable for copyright infringement by solely providing the means for the telecommunication or reproduction of the work through the Internet.

[27] Chwelos, P. 'Internet Service Providers Report', Prepared for Industry Canada, 2006, available at: http://www.ic.gc.ca/eic/site/ippd-dppi.nsf/eng/ip01437.html?Open&pv=1

[28] See Telus' description of the voluntary agreement in its consultation response, available at: http://balancedcopyright.gc.ca/eic/site/crp-prda.nsf/eng/rp00245.html

[29] Section 2.3 of the Copyright Modernization Act.

[30] See http://www.ic.gc.ca/eic/site/crp-prda.nsf/eng/rp01184.html

[31] See Section 46.(1) of the Copyright Modernization Act which replaces Subsections 38.1(1) to (3) of the Act with "38(1.11) For the purpose of subsection (1), an infringement under subsection 27(2.3) is deemed to be for a commercial purpose."

[32] Copyright Act, R.S.C., 1985, c. C-42, current to May 1, 2014, available at: http://laws-lois.justice.gc.ca/eng/acts/C-42/. Hereafter referred to as "the Copyright Act".

[33] Copyright Modernization Act, available at: http://www.parl.gc.ca/HousePublications /Publication.aspx?Language=E&Mode=1&DocId=5697419&File=4&Col=1 and http://laws-lois.justice.gc.ca/eng/annualstatutes/2012_20/FullText.html. Hereafter referred to as "the Copyright Modernization Act".

[34] A similar Act ('An Act to Amend the Copyright Act, Bill C-32') had been put forward in 2010 and was reviewed in parliament, but was not passed before Parliament was dissolved after the 2011 no-confidence motion.

[35] Safe harbour provisions for information location tools are specified under section 41.27 of the Copyright Act.

[36] According to the Copyright Act, where copyright has been infringed, the infringer must pay damages to the copyright owner equivalent to the losses suffered as a result of the infringement and any profits the infringer may have made following use of the infringed

material. Section 35.(1) of the Copyright Act "*Where a person infringes copyright, the person is liable to pay such damages to the owner of the copyright as the owner has suffered due to the infringement and, in addition to those damages, such part of the profits that the infringer has made from the infringement and that were not taken into account in calculating the damages as the court considers just.*"

[37] As explained by Industry Canada at http://www.ic.gc.ca/eic/site/crp-prda.nsf/eng/h_rp01153.html#concern

[38] Section 41.26 (3) of the Copyright Modernization Act, "A claimant's remedy against a person who fails to perform his or her obligations...is statutory damages in an amount that the court considers just, but not less that $5,000 and no more than $10,000."

[39] Section 41.26 (4) of the Copyright Modernization Act.

[40] 41.25(2) of the Copyright Modernization Act.

[41] Section 18 of the Copyright Modernization Act amending Section 27 subsection (2) of the Copyright Act.

[42] Chwelos, P. 'Internet Service Providers Report', Prepared for Industry Canada, 2006, available at: http://www.ic.gc.ca/eic/site/ippd-dppi.nsf/eng/ip01437.html?Open&pv=1

[43] See: http://www.parl.gc.ca/HousePublications/Publication.aspx?DocId=5057232 &Language=E&Mode=1&Parl=40&Ses=3

[44] Namely Claro, Deezer, Google Play Music, Imusica, Itunes, Kboing, Mercado Da Musica, Mixradio, Mundo Oi, Music Unlimited, Power Music Club, Rara.Com, Rdio, Spotify, Terra Musica Powered By Napster, Tim, Toing, Uol Megastore, Vevo, Vivo Musica By Napster, Xbox Music, Yahoo Musica, Youtube

[45] It is not clear how APCM arrived at the identification of these sites.

[46] ARCEP Quarterly report: http://www.arcep.fr/index.php?id=8571&L=1&tx_gsactualite_pi1[uid]=1702&tx_
gsactualite_pi1[annee]=&tx_gsactualite_pi1[theme]=&tx_gsactualite_pi1[motscle]=&tx_gsactualite_ pi1[backID]=26&cHash=25464e2275afbc2b3cabb530054827d3

[47] Including: 121 Music Store, 7Digital, Altermusique, Amazonmp3, Beatport, Cd1D, Daily Motion, Deezer, Echopolite, Emusic, Ezic, Fnac Jukebox, Google Play, Itunes, Jamendo, Jazz En Ligne, Last Fm, Mixradio, Music Unlimited, Musicme, Musicovery, My Clubbing Store, Mysurround, Napster, Qobuz, Rara.Com, Rdio, Sfr Music, Spotify, Starzik, Vevo, Vidzone, Virgin Mega, Xbox Music, Youtube, Zaoza,

[48] All statistics taken from the reporting of the Harris Interactive surveys in HADOPI (2014) HADOPI Annual Report 2014.

[49] «Loi n° 2006-961 du 1 août 2006 relative au droit d'auteur et aux droits voisins dans la société de l'information », available at : http://www.legifrance.gouv.fr/affichTexte.do?cidTexte=JORFTEXT000000266350

[50] HADOPI, '2010 Activity Report', November 2011. Available at: http://hadopi.fr/sites/default/files/page/pdf/Hadopi_Rapportannuel_ENG.pdf

[51] «LOI n° 2009-669 du 12 juin 2009 favorisant la diffusion et la protection de la création sur internet», available at: http://www.legifrance.gouv.fr/affichTexte.do?cidTexte= JORFTEXT000020735432&categorieLien=id

[52] «LOI n° 2009-1311 du 28 octobre 2009 relative à la protection pénale de la propriété littéraire et artistique sur internet», available at : http://www.legifrance.gouv.fr/affichTexte.do?cidTexte=JORFTEXT000021208046&categorieLien=id

[53] This is a principle that was originally established in the French legal system in the 2006 "Act for Copyright and Neighbouring Rights in the Information Society" « Loi n° 2006-961 du 1 août 2006 relative au droit d'auteur et aux droits voisins dans la société de l'information »,

available at: http://www.legifrance.gouv.fr/affichTexte. do?cidTexte=JORFTEXT 000000 266350

[54] Journal officiel "Lois et Décrets" - JORF n°0056 du 7 mars 2010, 'Décret n° 2010-236 du 5 mars 2010' available at: http://www.legifrance.gouv.fr/affichJO.do?idJO=JORF CONT 000021923812

[55] Article L. 336-2 of the French Intellectual Property Code, « LOI n° 2009-669 du 12 juin 2009 favorisant la diffusion et la protection de la création sur internet »

[56] While this exists, 'notice and take down' actions are currently largely ineffective in France, see 'Contextual and contributory factors' below

[57] Article L. 331-13 of the French Intellectual Property Code, « LOI n° 2009-669 du 12 juin 2009 favorisant la diffusion et la protection de la création sur internet »

[58] The SACEM (Société des auteurs, compositeurs et éditeurs de musique), the ALPA (Association de lutte contre la piraterie audiovisuelle), the SCPP (Société Civile des Producteurs Phonographique) and the SPPF (Société Civile des Producteurs de Phonogrammes en France).

[59] HADOPI, '2010 Activity Report', November 2011. Available at: http://hadopi.fr/sites/default /files/page/pdf/Hadopi_Rapportannuel_ENG.pdf

[60] LESCURE Pierre, 'Mission Acte II de l'exception culturelle, Contributions aux politiques culturelles à l'ère numérique – Tome 1', Ministry of Culture and Communication, May 2013, p. 359.

[61] HADOPI, « Descriptif du système mis en place par les ayants droit français (cinéma et musique) pour réaliser les constats d'infractions transmis à l'Hadopi »

[62] HADOPI sends this first notification to subscribers by email through their ISP, which means that this is often not read due to users using other email services. HADOPI, '2010 Activity Report', November 2011, p. 36.

[63] See IP news article «France: Analyse de la Decision Allostreaming» http://www.ipnews.be /france-analyse-de-la-decision-allostreaming/

[64] See Commentçamarche.net article «The Pirate Bay: Les entreprises françaises du disque veulent bloquer son accès » http://www.commentcamarche.net/news/5864587-the-pirate-bay-les-entreprises-francaises-dudisque-veulent-bloquer-son-acces

[65] Journal officiel "Lois et Décrets" - JORF n°0157 du 9 juillet 2013, 'Décret n° 2013-596 du 8 juillet 2013' available at: http://www.legifrance.gouv.fr/affichJO.do;jsessionid= DDF622129777D37347A492CDEFCD6000. tpdjo09v_3?idJO=JORFCONT000027677981

[66] The notifications that HADOPI send to subscribers do not disclose this information as this is intended to guarantee the privacy of individual internet users as the notifications are not addressed to the user guilty of copyright infringement but to the internet subscriber, who may be unaware of the activities behind the act of infringement. Subscribers can, however, receive the detailed information in the claim from the CMO if they request it.

[67] HADOPI, "Réponse graduée – Les chiffres clés", June 2014. Available at : http://www.hadopi.fr/sites/default/files/ChiffresRGjuin14.pdf

[68] See Le Monde news Article «Le seul internaute condamné par Hadopi passe à travers les mailles du filet» http://www.lemonde.fr/technologies/article/2013/09/05/l-unique-condamne-a-une-coupure-internet-voit-sa-peine-annulee_3472129_651865.html

[69] HADOPI, 'Press Briefing: Rights Protection Commission, Key figures of the graduated response', 16 July 2014, p. 2.

[70] Danaher, B, Smith, M.D., Telang, R. and Chen, S. (2013) 'The Effect of Graduated Response Anti-Piracy Laws on Music Sales. Evidence from an Event Study in France', forthcoming in *The Journal of Industrial Economics*.

[71] In particular, the control group used in the study is heterogeneous – meaning that it is unlikely that the underlying assumption that the only difference between the control group and France is the Hadopi law holds true. Also, the moment used as the difference-in-difference cut-off is a bit surprising, as the authors used the moment the law was presented in the National Assembly. Logically it would make more sense to either use the moment that the law is approved, or when Hadopi started to implement its policy. This is particularly relevant as the core of the results appear to happen between the initial discussion and the approval of the law, not after its actual implementation. Finally, it should also be pointed out that the study only covers the (self-reported) sales of four major labels on iTunes. This might create an additional problem for the use of the control group as the relative importance of iTunes might be very different across the studied countries.

[72] This has been confirmed by the three stakeholders interviewed by this research, Confindustria Digitale (CD), SIAE and AGCOM.

[73] Marzia Minozzi, Resp. Affari Istituzionali e Regolamentari di Assotelecomunicazioni Asstel, 16/06/2014, pers. comm.; Maja Cappello, Dirigente dell'Ufficio diritti digitali della Direzione Servizi media, 17/06/2014, pers. comm.; Paolo Agoglia,direttore dell'ufficio legislativo SIAE, 20/06/2014, pers. comm.

[74] AGCOM (2014). Indagine Conoscitiva sulla concorrenza statica e dinamica nel mercato dei servizi accesso e sulle prospettive di investimento nelle reti di telecomunicaxioni a banda larga e ultra larga, available at: http://www. agcm.it/trasp-statistiche/doc_download/4514-ic-48-testo-integale.html, p.26

[75] Ibid, p. 26

[76] 2012 data from the International Telecommunications Union, as presented in Figure 1 above.

[77] AGCOM (2014), Op. Cit, p. 27

[78] Ibid, p. 29

[79] AGCOM (2010). *Indagine Conosctiva: Diritto D'Autore sulle Reti di Comunicazione Elettronica,* available at: http://www.agcom.it/documents/10179/539311/Documento+Generico+12-02-2010/02bf7d56-3a36-4f3c-b9e8- abd900d8269b?version=1.0

[80] Marzia Minozzi, Resp. Affari Istituzionali e Regolamentari di Assotelecomunicazioni Asstel, 16/06/2014, pers. comm.;

[81] IFPI (2013), Digital Music Report 2012 Motore dell'universo digitale, Versione Italiana a cura di FIMI, PMI and Kiver Digital, available at: http://www.ifpi.org/downloads /dmr2013_italian.pdf

[82] Ibid, p. 19

[83] Bennato, D. And others (2007). *I comportamenti di consumo dei contenuti digitali in Italia, il caso del filesharing*, Roma: Fondazione Luigi Einaudi

[84] Marzia Minozzi, Resp. Affari Istituzionali e Regolamentari di Assotelecomunicazioni Asstel, 16/06/2014, pers. comm.; Maja Cappello, Dirigente dell'Ufficio diritti digitali della Direzione Servizi media, 17/06/2014, pers. comm.; Paolo Agoglia,direttore dell'ufficio legislativo SIAE, 20/06/2014, pers. comm.

[85] FAPAV-Ipsos (2009). *La pirateria AudioVisiva in Italia,* available at: http://www.fapav.it/1/osservatorio/1/; FAPAV- ipsos (2011). *La pirateria Audiovisiva in Italia*, seconda indagine conoscitiva, available at: http://www.fapav.it/1/ osservatorio/1/

[86] In 2008, the Music Piracy Federation, FPM, highlighted that at least 23% of online users were illegally downloading music through P2P and estimated that an average of 1300 songs was downloaded for every PC equipped with P2P software. FAPAV and Ipsos conducted two studies about audiovisual piracy in 2009 and 2011. According to their findings, audiovisual piracy is significantly and increasingly widespread in Italy, with more than 80% of films

available as early as two days after release in film theatres. Moreover, the 2011 study showed an increasing trend in the diffusion of audio-visual piracy.

[87] IIPA (2012). 2012 *Special 301 Report on Copyright Protection and Enforcement*, p. 187, available at: http://www.iipa.com/rbc/2012/2012SPEC301ITALY.PDF

[88] IIPA (2013). 2013 *Special 301 Report on Copyright Protection and Enforcement*, available at: http://www.iipa.com/rbc/2013/2013SPEC301ITALY.PDF

[89] See Spotify (2013). *Adventures in the Netherlands: Spotify, Piracy and the new Dutch experience*; TERA consultants (2011). *Building A Digital Economy: The Importance of Saving Jobs in the EU's Creative Industries*; AGCOM (2010) op. cit.; IIPA (2010). 2010 *Special 301 Report on Copyright Protection and Enforcement*, available at: http://www.iipa.com/rbc/2010/2010SPEC301ITALY.pdf; IIPA (2011). 2011 *Special 301 Report on Copyright Protection and Enforcement, available at*: http://www.iipa.com/rbc/2011/2011SPEC301ITALY.pdf; IIPA (2012),op. cit.

[90] FAPAV-Ipsos (2009) op. cit.

[91] Rego, D. P. (2013). *Hello Italy, Poland and Portugal. Spotify here*.available at: http://news.spotify.com/uk/2013/02/12/hello-italy-poland-portugal/

[92] AGCOM Resolution 21st Jan 2014, n. 27/14/CONS

[93] Maja Cappello,Dirigente dell'Ufficio diritti digitali della Direzione Servizi media, 17/06/2014, pers. comm.

[94] Marzia Minozzi, Resp. Affari Istituzionali e Regolamentari di Assotelecomunicazioni Asstel, 16/06/2014, pers. comm.

[95] Paolo Agoglia,direttore dell'Ufficio Legislativo SIAE, 20/06/2014, pers. comm.

[96] Namely 7Digital, Countdownload, Deezer, Downloadmusic, Emusic, Glandigomusic, Google Play, Itunes, Jamba, Juke, Last Fm, Legal Download, Mixradio, Msn Nl, Mtv, Music Unlimited, Muziekweb, Napster, Qobuz, Radio 538, Rara.Com, Rdio, Spotify, Talpadownloads, Tunetribe, Vevo, Vidzone, Xbox Music, You Make Music, Youtube, Zazell.Nl, Ziggo Muziek

[97] SEO, IViR and CentERdata (2012) *Digitale drempels, Knelpunten voor legaal digitaal aanbod in de creatieve industrie*.

[98] Poort, J. and J. Leenheer; Filesharing 2012, *Downloaden in Nederland*, IViR and CentERdata, 2012. http://www.ivir.nl/publicaties/poort/Filesharing_2012.pdf and Leenheer, J. and J. Poort; "*Alleen maar nette mensen" Consumentenonderzoek Downloadgedrag Films*, IViR and CentERdata, 2014. In Dutch: http://www.ivir.nl/ publicaties/poort/alleen_maar_nette_ mensen.pdf

[99] For instance, the Amsterdam Internet Exchange (AMS-IX) is the 2nd largest Internet Exchange worldwide in terms of traffic (bits per second) and the Netherlands scores 6th place globally on broadband penetration - 'Digital Infrastructure in the Netherlands: The Third Mainport", Peters, M., A. van Dijk, S. Ward (Deloitte), November 2013, to be found: http://ecp.nl/item/3937.

[100] Arguments focused on the legality of bit torrent and UseNet-sites, as well as questions such as whether hosting providers should take these types of sites offline, whether sites should use filters to prevent linking to unlawful content, whether hosting providers should be forced to provide information about the person or organisation behind an anonymous website, whether hosting providers should provide information about uploaders of unlawful material and who would bear the costs of all these actions. A lot of information about the legal battles can be found by entering BREIN, rechtszaak (lawsuit) and a specific year in a search engine, for example: https://www. google.nl/#q=brein+rechtzaak+2008

[101] A very vocal opponent was and is the internet provider Xs4all that states that filters are very easy to work around, they will also block legal content, they lay a heavy burden on ISPs in terms of service and costs and are actually a form of censorship and limit the freedom of speech. This view can be found here (in Dutch) https://www.xs4all.nl/media/maatschappelijk/standpuntxs4all.pdf. An important NGO in this field, is Bits of Freedom, Dutch digital rights organization, "focusing on privacy and communications freedom in the digital age".

[102] A working group has been established to monitor the workings of the code and prepare updates. The description of the Code of Conduct on information from this working group (http://ecp.nl/werkgroep-notice-and-takedown) and from a factsheet about the legal implications of the Code of Conduct for ISP's (https://ictrecht.nl/factsheets/ notice-and-takedown/).

[103] The initiative for the NTD Code was taken by the two largest associations of internet service providers, the association of cable companies and a number of individual ISPs. The NTD Code was also realised with the support and input of a number of public organisations and private internet-related parties.

[104] The Netherlands has a copy levy system where importers or manufacturers of recording media and/or equipment are liable for payment. The Court ruled that the Dutch levy system was not in accordance with the European directive (2001/29/EG). This was because the Dutch levy regulation does not distinguish between lawful and unlawful downloads. In fact, according to the EU Court of Justice, the Dutch levy regulation compensates for illegal downloads. Ruling in Dutch: http://curia.europa.eu/jcms/upload/docs/application/ pdf/2014-04/cp140058nl.pdf, in English: http://curia.europa.eu/juris/document/document. jsf?text=&docid=150786&pageIndex=0&doclang=EN&mode=lst&dir=&occ=first&part=1&cid=363923

[105] Letter of the Ministry of Security and Justice to parliament, dated 17th of April, in Dutch: http://www.rijksoverheid. nl/nieuws/2014/04/17/kabinet-stuurt-brief-over-downloaden-uit-illegale-bron.html

[106] Quote from a BREIN press release published immediately after the court ruling, published on April 10th, 2014 (in Dutch): http://anti-piracy.nl/nieuws.php?id=322

[107] All in Dutch, amendments: http://wetten.overheid.nl/BWBR0016987, and the Copy Right Act: http://wetten. overheid.nl/BWBR0001886

[108] Neighbouring Rights Act (in Dutch): http://wetten.overheid.nl/BWBR0005921

[109] The Public Prosecutor's Office formulates instructions that determine the way in which the office implements its enforcement policy. There is a specific set of instructions regarding infringement of intellectual property right. The line of reasoning in the instruction is as follows: infringement of intellectual property rights should in principle be a matter of enforcement under civil law by the rights holders themselves. Exceptions to this, when the Prosecutor's Office should prosecute under criminal law, relate to: (i) large scale piracy on a professional or commercial basis that leads to market distortion (ii) the involvement of organised crime in the infringement of intellectual property rights; and (ii) repeat offending.

[110] The Fiscal Information and Investigation Service (Fiscale inlichtingen- en opsporingsdienst, FIOD), that exists under the Ministry of Finance, has a task in investigating economic offences and prosecuting these before a fiscal or criminal court. But these cases rarely concern online infringement. The FIOD targets large scale infringements of IP that distorts markets. Smaller cases are handled by the police (for example: illegal copying or trading from homes or on markets). If a small amount of illegal merchandise is confiscated, and the suspect is prepared to surrender the merchandise, the Prosecutors Office can settle the case

with a fine and without further prosecution (http://www.anti-piracy.nl/vormen-van-inbreuk.phpj (in Dutch).

[111] Under Dutch law, intermediaries are not legally obligated to know and maintain a record of the names and contact details of their clients.

[112] http://wetten.overheid.nl/BWBR0001886

[113] The category of the fine and the corresponding amount in Euro's, are official yearly publications, and can be found on: http://www.rijksoverheid.nl/onderwerpen/straffen-en-maatregelen/vraag-en-antwoord/hoe-hoog-zijn-deboetes-in-nederland.html

[114] In Dutch: http://anti-piracy.nl/nieuws.php?id=320

[115] McAfee Labs Threat s Report, June 2014: http://www.mcafee.com/uk/resources/reports/rp-quarterlythreat-q1-2014.pdf

[116] http://webwereld.nl/e-commerce/82964-xs4all-weer-gedagvaard-door-brein-wegens-pirate-bay

[117] Cultural prosperity' is largely defined as (1) 'cultural prosperity': enhancement of overall capacity of the cultural and creative sector; and (2) 'prosperity through culture': contribution of cultural and creative sector to other social sectors

[118] National copyright industry standard classifications (Nov. 8, 2011) – Core copyright industries: industries fully engaged in the creation, production, manufacturing, performance, broadcast, communication, exhibition or distribution and sales of works and other protected objects.

[119] South Korea Copyright Commission COPY112 <www.copy112.or.kr>

[120] Illegal Copyright Obstruction Program (ICOP) automatically searches and gathers evidence of illegal reproductions, and requests suspension of reproduction/transmission of these materials to OSPs.

[121] KCC is the sole governmental agency dedicated to copyright-related affairs established in 2009 by Article 112 of the Copyright Act. Its main responsibilities are deliberating copyright-related issues, mediating copyright disputes, researching policies and legislation on copyright, copyright education and public awareness PR, and serves as a copyright registration agency.

[122] Copyright Commission Annual Report 2012. P. 29

[123] MCST 2013 Budget <www.mcst.go.kr>

[124] CPC Annual Report 2013, p.101,

[125] http://www.boe.es/boe/dias/2011/03/05/pdfs/BOE-A-2011-4117.pdf

[126] https://www.eff.org/deeplinks/2012/01/spains-ley-sinde-new-revelations

[127] This is produced annually by the Office of the United States Trade Representative (USTR) and the reports highlight any trade barriers to US companies that exist in different countries due to their intellectual property laws (or the enforcement therein of their laws).

[128] http://www.cadenaser.com/cultura/articulo/supone-ley-sinde/csrcsrpor/20101221csrcsrcul_2/Tes

[129] http://www.cityoflondon.police.uk/advice-and-support/fraud-and-economic-crime/pipcu/pipcu-news/Pages/ PIPCU-goes-global-in-its-pursuit-of-illegal-websites.aspx

[130] Defined by Ofcom as those with headline speeds of 30Mbit/s or more.

[131] See Ofcom, "The European Broadband Scorecard", 12 March 2014. Available at: http://stakeholders.ofcom.org.uk/binaries/research/broadband-research/scorecard/European_Broadband_Scorecard_2014.pdf

[132] Figures are based on end 2013 data for fixed (wired)-broadband subscriptions as published in the "18th edition of the World Telecommunication/ICT Indicators Database"; International

Telecommunication Union, 2014. Available at: http://www.itu.int/en/ITU-D/Statistics/Pages/stat/default.aspx.

[133] Including, Netflix, Itunes (music, movies, TV shows), Amazon Streaming, Youtube, Google Play (Movies, TV Shows, music), Spotify.

[134] http://www.ifpi.org/about.php

[135] Including: 7digital, Amazing Tunes, AmazonMP3, ArtistXite, Beatport, Bleep, Blinkbox, Bloom.fm, Boomkat, Classical.com, Classical Archives, Classics Online, Coolroom, Deezer, Drum & Bass Arena, eMusic, Fairsharemusic, Google Play, Highresaudio, Historic Recordings, HMV Digital, Imodownload, iTunes, Jamster, Jango, Junodownload, last.fm, Linn Records, MixRadio (Nokia), Mobile Chilli, MSN, MTV, Music Unlimited, Musicovery, MUZU.TV, My Music Anywhere, MySpace, Napster, Naxos, Nectar Music Store, O2 , Orange, Play. com, Pure Music, Psonar, Qobuz, rara.com, Rdio, Rokomobile, Sainsburys, , Spotify, The Classical Shop, Tidal, trackitdown, Traxsource, TuneTribe, Vevo, Vidzone, Virgin Media, Xbox Music, Yahoo! Music, Yondermusic, YouTube.

[136] Kantar media had been selected by the IPO and Ofcom to provide regular reports in the form of the Copyright Infringemnt Tracker. However, Wave 4 was the last survey before funding stopped.

[137] Available at: http://stakeholders.ofcom.org.uk/market-data-research/other/telecoms-research /oci-wave4/

[138] See page 29 of Copyright Infringement Tracker, Wave 4, Kantar Media, September 2013. Available at: http:// stakeholders.ofcom.org.uk/market-data-research/other/telecoms-research/oci-wave4/

[139] Copyright Infringement Tracker, Wave 4, Kantar Media, September 2013. Available at: http://stakeholders.ofcom. org.uk/market-data-research/other/telecoms-research/oci-wave4/

[140] A further condition for hosting providers to escape liability is that they have no knowledge of unlawful activity, and are not aware of facts that would have made it apparent that unlawful activity took place, or the material hosted infringed copyright (Section 19 (1) of the Electronic Commerce (EC Directive) Regulations 2002).

[141] Directive 2001/29/EC of the European Parliament and of the Council of 22 May 2001 on the harmonisation of certain aspects of copyright and related rights in the information society.

[142] Section 4Aofthe CDPA 1988 http://www.legislation.gov.uk /ukpga/1988/48/section/107#commentary-c1935540

[143] See http://www.cityoflondon.police.uk/advice-and-support/fraud-and-economic-crime/pipcu /pipcu- news /Pages/Advert-replacement.aspx

[144] Page 55, "Digital Economy Act 2010 Impact Assessments", BIS, IPO, DCMS, April 2010.

[145] Page 77, "Digital Economy Act 2010 Impact Assessments", BIS, IPO, DCMS, April 2010.

[146] Annex 7, of "Online infringement of Copyright: Implementation of the Online Infringement of Copyright (Initial Obligations) (Sharing of Costs) Order 2012", Ofcom Consultation, 26 June 2012.

[147] Twentieth Century Fox and others v British Telecommunications PLC 2011. Judgment available at: http://www. bailii.org/ew/cases/EWHC/Ch/2011/1981.html

[148] Page 44, IP Crime Group Annual Report 2012-2013, available at: http://www.ipo.gov.uk/pro-policy/pro-crime/ pro-crime-report.htm

[149] IP Crime highlight report 2013/14 reported that PRS for Music successfully removed 73,333 files during 2013, embodying 2,339,118 infringed musical works and the BPI removed 72,000,000 links to infringing digital material. Available at: https://www.gov.uk/government/uploads/system/uploads/attachment_data/file/318338/IP_crime_highlight_report.PDF

150 http://www.cityoflondon.police.uk/advice-and-support/fraud-and-economic-crime/pipcu/pipcu-news/Pages/City-of-London-Police-call-for-help-tackle-cyber-crime.aspx

151 http://www.cityoflondon.police.uk/advice-and-support/fraud-and-economic-crime/pipcu/pipcu-news/Pages/280514-illegal-websites-suspended.aspx

152 http://www.cityoflondon.police.uk/advice-and-support/fraud-and-economic-crime/pipcu/pipcu-news/Pages/ PIPCU-anniversary.aspx

153 At the mitigation alert stage a subscriber will receive alert noting that they "may be subject to a lawsuit for copyright infringement by the Copyright Owners and that continued infringement may, in appropriate circumstances, result in the imposition of action consistent with section 512 of the DMCA ... including temporary suspension or termination." See section 4(G) of the MOU.

154 See "2014 Measuring Broadband America Report on Fixed Broadband", FCC, 2 April 2014. Available at http:// www.fcc.gov/reports/measuring-broadband-america-2014

155 The report focused on four ISP delivery technologies (DSL, cable, fiber, and satellite) and examined offerings from the largest broadband providers, which together accounted for over 80 percent of U.S. residential broadband connections. The reports focussed on broadband performance during the peak usage period (defined as weeknights between 7:00 pm to 11:00 pm).

156 Figures are based on end 2013 data for fixed (wired)-broadband subscriptions as published in the "18th edition of the World Telecommunication/ICT Indicators Database"; International Telecommunication Union, 2014. Available at: http://www.itu.int/en/ITU-D/Statistics/Pages/stat/default.aspx.

157 Including, Netflix, Itunes (music, movies, TV shows), Amazon Streaming, Youtube, Google Play (Movies, TV Shows, music), Spotify.

158 Page 5 of the CCI's First Annual Review.

159 http://www.ifpi.org/about.php

160 Including: 7digital, Acoustic Sounds, AmazonMP3, AOL Radio Plus, Arkiv Music, ArtistXite, AT&T Wireless, Beatport, Beats Music, CD Universe, ChristianBook.com, Classical Archives, Cricket, Daily Motion, Deezer, Free All Music, Freegal Music, Ghosttunes, Google Play, Guvera, Hastings, Hdtracks, Hoopla, Hulu, Insound, iOldies, iTunes, iTunes Radio, MetroPCS, Mixradio, MTV, Music Choice, Music Unlimited, MusicGivz, Muve Music, TheOverflow, Pro Studio Masters, Qello, rara.com, Rdio, Rhapsody, Rokomobile, Slacker, Spotify, Sprint, T-Mobile, Verizon Wireless, Vidzone, Vevo, Virgin Mobile, Xbox Music, Yahoo! Music, YouTube, Yonder music, ZUUS.

161 Page 3 of the CCI's First Annual Review.

162 Page 3 of the CCI's First Annual Review.

163 Page 5 of the CCI's First Annual Review. Available at: http://www.copyrightinformation.org/wp-content/uploads/2014/05/Phase-One-And_Beyond.pdf

164 Page 5 of the CCI's First Annual Review, where it also reports that, "...if we look over the past decade, digital music download sales in the U.S. grew over 1400% from $183 million to $2.8 billion, with over 30 million tracks available online today."

165 The survey took into account a general cross-section of the U.S. Internet-using population between the ages of 13 and 59. Page 5 of the CCI's First Annual Review.

166 See https://futureofmusic.org/article/full-summary-digital-millennium-copyright-act

167 including Internet Service Providers and other internet intermediaries.

168 Section 202 of the DMCA inserting §512(c)(1)(A) into the United States Code.

169 According to Section 202 of the DMCA inserting §512(i)(1)(A) into the United States Code, the service provider must have "adopted and reasonaly implemented, and informs

subscriber and account holders of the service provider's system or network of, a policy that provides for the termination in appropriate circumstances of subscribers and account holders of the service provider's system who are repeat infringers".

[170] Section 202 of the DMCA, inserting §512 (h)(3) into the United States Code.

[171] For a full list of members, see the signatories of the CCI's 'Memorandum of Understanding, Final, 7/6/2011' available at http://www.copyrightinformation.org/wp-content/uploads/2013/02/Memorandum-ofUnderstanding.pdf (Hereafter referred to as the MOU).

[172] See http://www.copyrightinformation.org/about-cci/

[173] Section 202 of the DMCA, inserting §512(c)(1) into the United States Code.

[174] See Section 202 of the DMCA inserting §512(d)

[175] Title 17 of the United States Code § 504(b).

[176] Title 17 of the United States Code § 504(c).

[177] Title 17 of the United States Code § 504(c)(2).

[178] Section 4(G)(iii) of the MOU on the 'Mitigation Measure Step'. Note that "Participating ISPs shall not be obligated to apply a Mitigation Measure that knowingly disables or is reasonably likely to disable a Subscriber's access to any IP voice service (including over-the-top IP voice service), e-mail account, or any security service, multichannel video programming distribution service or guide, or health service (such as home security or medical monitoring) while a Mitigation Measure is in effect."

[179] Section 202 of the DMCA inserting §512(c)(3) into the United States Code.

[180] Sections 4(A) and 4(D) of the MOU.

[181] In the case that the independent expert/s *"find the methodology to be fundamentally unreliable, the Independent Expert shall issue a confidential finding of inadequacy ("Finding of Inadequacy") to the affected Content Owner Representative to permit the affected Content Owner Representative to modify or change the Methodology for review."* Section 4(B) of the MOU.

[182] Section 2 of the Second Amendment to the MOU.

[183] Section 2(E) of the MOU.

[184] Page 1 of the CCI, 'The Copyright Alert System, Phase one and beyond', May 2014 (herafter referred to as "the CCI's First Annual Review". Available at: http://www.copyrightinformation.org/wp-content/uploads/2014/05/Phase-One-And_Beyond.pdf

[185] Page 8 of the CCI's First Annual Review.

In: International Approaches ...
Editor: Patricia Wade
ISBN: 978-1-63483-168-0

Chapter 2

2014 Out-of-Cycle Review of Notorious Markets*

United States Trade Representative

Results of the 2014 Out-of-Cycle Review of Notorious Markets

Overview

Commercial scale trademark counterfeiting and copyright piracy cause significant financial losses for rights holders and legitimate businesses, undermine critical U.S. comparative advantages in innovation and creativity to the detriment of American workers, and can pose significant risks to consumer health and safety. The Notorious Markets List ("List") highlights select online and physical marketplaces that reportedly engage in and facilitate substantial copyright piracy and trademark counterfeiting.[1]

The Office of the United States Trade Representative ("USTR") has developed the List under the auspices of the annual Special 301 process.[2] USTR solicited comments regarding which markets to highlight in this year's List through a *Request for Public Comments* published in the *Federal Register* (*www.regulations.gov*, Docket Number USTR-2014-0017).

---

* This is an edited, reformatted and augmented version of a report issued March 5, 2015.

The List is based on publicly-available information. USTR selected markets not only because they exemplify global concerns about counterfeiting and piracy, but also because the scale of infringing activity in such markets can cause economic harm to U.S. IPR holders. Some of the identified markets reportedly host a combination of legitimate and unauthorized activities. Others reportedly exist solely to engage in or facilitate unauthorized activity. The List does not purport to be an exhaustive list of all physical and online markets worldwide in which IPR infringement takes place.

USTR has identified Notorious Markets in the Special 301 Report since 2006. In 2010, USTR announced that it would begin publishing the List separately from the annual Special 301 Report, pursuant to an Out-of-Cycle Review ("OCR"). USTR first separately published the List in February 2011. The present List is the result of the 2014 OCR of Notorious Markets.

The List does not purport to reflect findings of legal violations, nor does it reflect the U.S. Government's analysis of the general IPR protection and enforcement climate in the country concerned. A broader analysis of IPR protection and enforcement in particular countries or economies is presented in the annual Special 301 Report, published on or about April 30thof each year (please refer to the *Public Information* section at the end of this document).

The List repeats several previously-identified markets because our concerns with those particular markets have not been addressed. However, we examined each market anew and updated each listing. Other previously-identified markets may not appear in the present List for a variety of reasons, including that: the market has closed or its popularity or significance has diminished; enforcement or voluntary action has reduced or eliminated the prevalence of IPR-infringing goods or services; market owners or operators are cooperating with rights holders or government authorities to address infringement; the market is no longer the most noteworthy example of its kind; or no commenter nominated the market for continued inclusion on the List.

Positive Developments Since the 2013 Out-of-Cycle Review of Notorious Markets

Since the release of the 2013 List, some market owners and operators have made notable efforts to address the widespread availability of pirated or counterfeit goods in their markets. The United States commends these efforts, and encourages governments, rights holders, and the owners and operators of these and other markets, including those newly identified in the 2014 List, to engage in sustained and meaningful efforts to combat piracy and counterfeiting. For example, the operators of previously-listed *Seriesyonkis.com*[3] reportedly have taken voluntary action to reduce the availability of pirated content on the site following the commencement of criminal proceedings in Spain.[4] The operators of Aiseesoft.com voluntary ceased offering DVD and Blu-Ray "ripping" software after the site appeared in the 2013 List. Such welcome efforts can foster the development of legitimate marketplaces and business models, enhance consumer choice and security, and facilitate the next generation of creativity and innovation.

During the past year, some of the listed online markets undertook various measures that demonstrated a willingness to cooperate in addressing infringement, such as: providing streamlined notice and takedown procedures; expediting responses to complaints; completing licensing arrangements with rights holders; and engaging with rights holders to develop additional cooperative procedures. China's *Xunlei.com* ("Xunlei") has made several notable improvements since first being listed as a Notorious Market. In addition to shutting down its problematic affiliated service, *GouGou*, and transitioning *KanKan* to a legitimate format, Xunlei created a mechanism for reporting unauthorized content, and has entered into agreements with several rights holder organizations to distribute licensed content. However, USTR continues to receive complaints about Xunlei because the expected positive impact of at least some of those agreements with rights holder organizations is not yet apparent, and because Xunlei's broad efforts to date appear not to have effectively addressed the high level of unauthorized content that remains available. In recognition of Xunlei's efforts, and to encourage further improvement by Xunlei and by other Notorious Markets, USTR has removed Xunlei from the List for 2014. However, we will continue to monitor developments. USTR encourages sites such as Xunlei and listed site *Zing.vn* to deepen engagement with rights holders and to further ensure authorized use of content on their online markets.

In 2014, several previously-listed online markets closed or experienced disruption as a result of enforcement efforts. These include: *Wawa-mania.ec,* which was the focus of action by French authorities; *Kuaibo.com/QVOD* in China; and *Mp3skull.com* and *Share-rapid.cz,*[5] as a result of actions by the United Kingdom ("U.K.") and other governments as well as civil enforcement by rights holders.

In 2014, other previously-listed or nominated sites were the subject of significant domestic and international law enforcement efforts. Notable enforcement efforts occurred in Sweden, against *ThePirateBay.se*[6] and in

Germany, against the nominated but not listed site Boerse.bz (also operating as Kinox.to).[7] The Government of Spain also took significant enforcement action in 2014 against *Seriespepito.com* and *A Pedra Market*, a physical market in Vigo, Galicia. In addition, United States and European enforcement authorities cooperated in several enforcement actions against online markets, and the Italian Fiscal Police and Rome's public prosecutor joined forces against hundreds of sites delivering pirated content to Italian consumers. The United States commends these efforts and encourages trading partners to continue their individual and cooperative efforts to combat copyright piracy and trademark counterfeiting.

Putlocker.com was subject to various enforcement actions in 2012 and 2013. In 2014, the owner rebranded the cyberlocker as *Firedrive.com*, and reportedly continued to offer both streaming and downloading of unauthorized video files, including preserved Putlocker files. It is unclear whether the owner has maintained any of the anti-piracy controls previously instituted at *Putlocker.com,* or rather has returned to its past practices of improperly incentivizing and compensating users for illegal uploads. In any event, Firedrive's popularity has decreased dramatically from that of the original *Putlocker.com* site. Firedrive's Alexa.com[8] global rank of 9,842, is significantly lower than Putlocker's February 2014 global rank of 320. Due to this significant reduction in popularity, Putlocker/Firedrive is not listed this year.

Respondents to USTR's *Federal Register Request* describe Brazil's Camelodromo Uruguaiana (Rio de Janeiro) and Feira dos Importados (also known as Feira do Paraguai) (Brasilia) as being at the center of the country's trade in pirated video games and audiovisual products. Reportedly the largest shopping market in Rio de Janeiro, the Camelodromo Uruguaiana hosts over 1,500 kiosks, many of which sell pirated and counterfeit goods. Similarly, the Feira dos Importados offers apparel, fashion accessories, and toys, in addition to audiovisual entertainment products. Many of the counterfeit products sold there are reportedly produced in Asia. However, in contrast with the current situation described below at listed market *Galeria Page* (*Sao Paulo*), local authorities in both Brasilia and in Rio de Janeiro reportedly conduct regular enforcement actions at their markets. Also of note is that the enforcement actions in Brasilia and Rio de Janeiro receive press coverage, which promotes crucial public awareness. USTR applauds these efforts, and encourages Sao Paulo's authorities to resume previous levels of enforcement.

Additional positive developments in 2014 took the form of policy and commercial initiatives, as governments and businesses worldwide look for ways to address copyright piracy and trademark counterfeiting. For example, the Government of France continued its inclusive dialogue with stakeholders, resulting in another installment in a series of reports prepared for the Minister of Culture and Communications. Published in May 2014, *Operational Tools to Prevent and Combat Online Infringement*[9] included an informative review of the respective roles that participants in the Internet ecosystem can play in addressing, and developing alternatives to, online piracy. The report highlighted important voluntary initiatives that will be key to reducing online piracy while respecting the rights of law-abiding users. In the United States, a voluntary payment processor initiative,[10] launched as an outgrowth of the U.S. Intellectual Property Enforcement Coordinator's 2010 Strategic Plan, aims to address websites that persist in intentionally selling infringing products. Under the program, participating payment processors have terminated the accounts of nearly 4,000 online merchants. In Italy, a memorandum of understanding between online advertisers and the film and music industries is aimed at reducing or eliminating commercial advertising, the largest source of revenues for sites engaged in copyright piracy.[11]

Other Developments Related to Previously-Listed Markets

USTR continues to monitor markets that have been removed from the List. Markets may be re-listed if there is a change in circumstances, *e.g.*, if a website that ceased to operate as a result of enforcement or other action resumes its unauthorized activities or the corrective actions that merited removal from the List prove inadequate or short-lived.

A goal of the List is to motivate appropriate action on the part of owners and operators in the private sector as well as governments to reduce piracy and counterfeiting. In some cases, the situation in a particular market or geographic area presents unique challenges not effectively addressed in this OCR process.

While the situation in Ukraine has not improved in 2014, the political will to address specific IPR issues appears to have strengthened. The new administration, elected in October 2014, is undertaking efforts to reform the civil service and integrate competent civil society groups in the monitoring of Ukraine's ministries, courts, judiciary, and security services. However, a demonstrated, positive impact has yet to be seen in the IPR sphere. The sale of counterfeit and pirated products in previously-listed *Seventh Kilometer Market (Odessa),* and the newly-nominated Barabashova Market (Kharkiv) continues unabated. Rights holders did, however, comment positively on the enforcement efforts of Ukrainian officials at the previously-listed *Petrivka Market (Kyiv);* in recognition of this effort, the market is not listed. USTR encourages Ukrainian authorities to continue their efforts at Petrivka Market, including against "on demand" copying of copyright-protected content. USTR recognizes the particular challenges of enforcement at the Seventh Kilometer and Barabashova Markets, but caution against inaction.

The number of online markets reportedly operating in Ukraine and nominated for inclusion in the 2014 List increased relative to 2013. According to reports, the nominated sites are popular sources of unauthorized copyright-protected content in Ukraine and in dozens of countries worldwide. The proliferation of sites offering unauthorized content represents a complicated cybercrime and cybersecurity challenge for Ukrainian officials, and serves as a barrier to entry for legitimate providers that might otherwise consider offering products and services in Ukraine.[12] *Ex.ua* and *Extratorrent.cc* continue to appear in the List as illustrations of this problem.

The Chinese *website Taobao.com (*Alibaba Group) appeared in previous Lists for the widespread availability of counterfeit and pirated goods in its online market. USTR removed Taobao from the List in 2012 in recognition of efforts to address rights holder and consumer complaints. During the 2013 Notorious Markets review, Taobao provided assurances to various stakeholders that it would continue to work with all relevant stakeholders to address remaining issues. In particular, Taobao committed to address concerns raised by software, publishing, and apparel and footwear companies, many of which are small and medium-sized enterprises with limited enforcement resources. In response to the 2014 *Federal Register Request*, Alibaba Group informed USTR that the company, which owns Taobao and T-Mall, continued its efforts to address stakeholders' complaints, including by reportedly removing millions of listings for counterfeit and pirated products manufactured in China and offered for sale and export. In January 2015, the Chinese Government echoed several of the long-standing complaints against these markets in a report issued by the State Administration for Industry and Commerce (SAIC).[13] Press reports indicate that Alibaba and the Government of China will engage in a dialogue to address concerns raised in the SAIC report. In addition to the SAIC report, Taobao appeared in three of the top ten cases named by the National Copyright Administration of China in its 2014 "Sword Net Action Campaign." The three separate cases, involving pirated movies and other audiovisual products as well as software, are under the jurisdiction of local Ministries of Public Security in Jiangsu, Shandong, and

Hubei provinces. USTR is concerned about these developments but does not re-list Taobao at this time. USTR encourages the company to continue working with all stakeholders to address ongoing complaints, will continue to monitor the situation.

The two most notorious peer-to-peer sites associated with Bulgaria, *Zamunda.net* (also operating as *Zamunda.se* and previously as *Zelka.org*) and *Arenabg.com,* remain operational, offering pirated online movies, music, software, and video games, despite police and court action against them. The sites reportedly log thousands of unique entries (upload and download) daily by users from Bulgaria and the region. The appeal of a criminal conviction against Arenabg.com ended in 2013 with the acquittal of all four defendants, who initially had each been fined less than $700 by Sofia Regional Court. The latest trial involving Zamunda.net began in late 2014 in Sofia Regional Court. Although Bulgarian police have made meaningful efforts to take enforcement action against the operators of these markets, prosecutors and the courts have not yet been able to produce deterrent penalties against these operators. However, in recognition of Bulgarian law enforcement efforts[14] and recent reports that the operators of these sites agreed with rights holders to remove links to unauthorized movies upon notification, the sites are not listed below. USTR will continue to monitor this situation.

New Issue Focus: Domain Name Registrars

This year, USTR is highlighting the issue of certain domain name registrars. Registrars are the commercial entities or organizations that manage the registration of Internet domain names, and some of them reportedly are playing a role in supporting counterfeiting and piracy online.

In general, it is critical for rights holders to be able to enforce their rights, including through civil and administrative procedures, cooperation with law enforcement in criminal actions, and through the Internet Corporation for Assigned Names and Numbers' ("ICANN") procedures and policies.[15] However, the IPR enforcement system can break down when the tools available to rights holders become ineffective, due to, among other things, the failure of domain name registrars or other similarly situated entities to follow rules intended to help combat illicit activity.

The agreement between ICANN and domain name registrars[16] requires that registrars take action when notified of illicit activity occurring on a website whose domain name they have registered. Some registrars, however, reportedly disobey court orders and other communications, including from government enforcement authorities. Some registrars apparently even advertise to the online community that they will not take action against illicit activity, presumably to incentivize registrations by owners and operators of illicit sites. These entities reportedly refuse to abide by the rules that are designed to foster legitimate activity on the Internet, and instead help to create an atmosphere of lawlessness that adversely affects others, often profoundly.

Several respondents to the 2014 *Federal Register Request* identified registrars that purportedly facilitate the distribution of unauthorized copyright-protected content. One respondent identified several registrars that have apparently refused requests to lock or suspend domain names used to sell suspected counterfeit pharmaceuticals to consumers worldwide.[17] This conduct also presents a public health challenge, and requires a coordinated response by governments and a variety of private sector stakeholders.

According to one report, an estimated 96 percent of online pharmacies targeting U.S. consumers are operating in violation of applicable U.S. law and standards.[18] An estimated 50 percent of websites worldwide that hide their physical address are selling illicit pharmaceuticals,[19] including those labeled with counterfeit trademarks. The website *www.LegitScript.com* has reviewed over 40,000 online drug sellers, but found fewer than 400 to be legitimate. Studies have found that counterfeit anti-cancer, anti-HIV/AIDS, and other medications are not only ineffective, but in some cases may contain toxic or deadly adulterants, such as rat poison.[20]

With relatively few lawful sources amidst a sea of harmful ones, the public faces a substantial risk when navigating these online pharmaceutical markets. In addition to the public health and safety risks, there is also economic harm. Illegal online pharmaceutical sellers can generate significant revenues each month, diverting income from legitimate innovative and generic pharmaceutical manufacturers, and depriving governments of tax revenues from legitimate sales.

Registrars can play a critical public safety role in the Internet ecosystem. Ignoring that role, or acting affirmatively to facilitate public harm, is of great concern. One of the registrars nominated in response to USTR's *Federal Register Request*, *Tucows.com*, appears in the List below, as an example of this concern. USTR urges trading partner governments[21] and ICANN to investigate and address this very serious problem.

RESULTS OF THE 2014 OUT-OF-CYCLE REVIEW OF NOTORIOUS MARKETS

As noted, the List identifies particular online and physical markets in which pirated or counterfeit goods are reportedly available, but it does not constitute a legal finding or a conclusion as to IPR protection and enforcement in a host country or economy, nor is it intended to be an exhaustive listing of all notorious markets around the world. Rather, the List highlights some of the most prominent examples reported and examined during the OCR process.

Owners and operators of the Notorious Markets included in the 2014 List that are willing to address piracy and counterfeiting have many options for doing so. Such owners and operators can adopt business models that rely on the licensed distribution of legitimate content, and can negotiate appropriate licenses with rights holders. If an otherwise legitimate business has become a platform for piracy, the owner or operator can work with rights holders and enforcement officials to help curtail acts of infringement. However, in the absence of such good faith efforts, responsible government authorities should investigate reports of piracy and counterfeiting in these and similar markets, and pursue appropriate action against such markets and their owners and operators.

Online Markets[22]

The 2014 List of online markets again includes examples of various technologies and business models. USTR based its selections not on specific technologies or business models but on whether, based on available information, a nominated site or affiliated network of sites appears to engage in or facilitate IPR infringement. Accordingly, the 2014 List reflects nominations of sites that reportedly engage in copyright piracy and trademark counterfeiting as well as registrars that reportedly facilitate the distribution of pirated and counterfeit products, including medicines. In addition to facilitating IPR infringements, sites may lack safeguards for consumer privacy, security and safety, and some reportedly actively and surreptitiously install malware on users' computers.

4shared.com: With millions of unique visitors each day, this popular site, reportedly based in the British Virgin Islands, facilitates streaming and downloads of pirated videos, music, books and games. 4shared mobile apps further allow users to stream infringing content to their mobile devices. While this site has implemented a feature that scans for unauthorized content, the music industry reports that levels of infringement are substantial and continue to increase.

Baixeturbo.org: This long-running U.K.-hosted blog site has been operating since 2008, and is very popular in Brazil. The site reportedly specializes in infringing music but also offers unauthorized copies of films and television programs. The site is said to generate revenue from advertisements and the sale of premium accounts that allow linking to multiple cyberlockers[23] where users can download infringing files.

Bajui.com: While not popular on a global scale, for over five years Bajui, hosted in Canada, has reportedly been the source of allegedly infringing music made available to Spanish-speaking users through direct downloads. While rights holders have used Spain's new copyright law to take enforcement action against Bajui and an even more popular site, *Elitetorrent.com,* both have been able to evade effective enforcement by removing specific links included in complaints and replacing those links with new ones to the same allegedly infringing content. Bajui exemplifies the harm to music creators of pre-release piracy, while Elitetorrent provides links to unauthorized copies of movies and television programs.

Catshare.net: This Polish site reportedly offers unauthorized alternatives to multiplayer platforms, the gaming industry's latest business model. Sites such as this one, which reportedly offers unauthorized access to 36,000 infringing games, threaten the development of legitimate distribution models.

Cuevana.tv (*Storm*): In the last year, this Argentine site's operators have developed a new streaming application called "Cuevana Storm" that uses BitTorrent technology to allow users to stream allegedly infringing video content. Rights holders in the movie industry report that an attempt to take action against the site more than four years ago has stalled, leaving them without effective recourse.

Darkwarez.pl: Despite being highlighted in past Lists, Darkwarez reportedly continues to make available thousands of links to allegedly infringing video game content. The site targets Poland and Polish-speaking audiences.

Ex.ua and *Extratorrent.cc:* These sites, both of which have appeared on the List several times, continue to benefit from Ukraine's reported status as a haven for online piracy. Extratorrent allegedly has extremely high rates of piracy with over 1.4 million unauthorized files, tens of millions of users, and almost ten billion unique visits in a single month. While Extratorrent has been the subject of successful enforcement actions in the U.K., Italy, and Belgium, it maintains a global Alexa ranking of 345 and, notably, an Alexa ranking in India of 70, illustrating the commercial impact that sites which facilitate infringement can have on geographically diverse Movshare Group/Private Layer (operating as *Torrentz.eu*, Torrentz.me, Torrentz.ch, *Torrentz.in*, Putlocker.is, *Nowvideo.sx*, Movshare.net, Bitsnoop.com, *Novamov.com,* among others): This group of affiliated and extremely popular sites, with ties to Switzerland, Netherlands, Panama, Canada, and other countries, reportedly uses multiple technologies to make available countless unauthorized copies of movies, games, music, audiobooks, software, and sporting event broadcasts. The sites are said to generate revenues through advertising and membership or subscription fees, and compensate users for uploading infringing content. Switzerland has announced plans to close a loophole in its law that restricts enforcement against pirate sites. However, at this time, rights holders report that Switzerland is an increasingly popular host country for such sites.

Rutracker.org (formerly *Torrents.ru*) and *Rapidgator.net:* The operators of these sites that reportedly facilitate piracy have allegedly based their operations in Russia to evade *enforcement. Rutracker.org,* hosted in and operated from Russia, is the country's 17th most popular site, according to *Alexa.com*. Rapidgator, the popularity of which is declining, is hosted in Russia but primarily serves users outside of the country. Both of these sites have appeared in the List multiple times.

Tucows.com: Based in Canada,24 Tucows is reportedly an example of a registrar that fails to take action when notified of its clients' infringing activity.[25] Consistent with the discussion above, USTR encourages the operators of Tucows to work with relevant stakeholders to address complaints.

Ulozto.cz: This cyberlocker allegedly hosts and distributes more than 50 million files, many of which reportedly infringe copyrights in music and film. The site is most popular in the Czech Republic where it is hosted and has an Alexa ranking of 29. The music industry reports that attempts to work with Ulozto.cz to legitimize its business and develop a licensed music platform have failed.

Uploaded.net: This cyberlocker, with alleged connections to Switzerland and Netherlands, provides access to a broad range of unauthorized copies of copyright-protected materials, and reportedly generates over $6 million per year in advertising and subscription revenues. The site operator allegedly employs multiple IP addresses, domain names, and server locations to evade law enforcement.

vK.com (also known as *vKontakte.com*): Although its ownership has changed, *vK.com* has continued to operate as an extremely popular social networking site in Russia and neighboring countries. Social networking sites can serve as a uniquely valuable communication platform, enabling beneficial commercial, cultural, and social exchanges. Most successful social networking sites do so in ways that do not involve the active facilitation of copyright infringement. However, some site operators continue to generate revenues by enabling the unauthorized sharing of music and other content through their sites and associated software applications. vK's operators responded to the *Federal Register Request* with information about their anti-piracy efforts, but the reported continuing scope and volume of infringing content demonstrates that more needs to be done to yield positive change.

Yts.re (also known as *YIFY*): With millions of unique visitors each month and a rising global Alexa ranking in the low 700s, Yts.re is a popular site for allegedly pirated movies. Yts.re reportedly facilitates piracy through high quality movie downloads and evades enforcement through multiple IP addresses, and by basing its operations in multiple countries. Yts.re's operators also created a desktop torrent streaming application called "Popcorn Time," similar to "Cuevana Storm" (listed above). The "Popcorn Time" application mimics popular legitimate subscription-based streaming services but, instead of authorized films, users download reportedly infringing movies using BitTorrent technology and can further distribute the infringing content to others. While the original "Popcorn Time" application may no longer be available, spin-offs—or "forks"—of the application continue to be developed under variations of the popular "Popcorn Time" name.

Yyets.com (operating as *Zimuzu.tv*): Described by some commenters as the most popular dedicated website for copyright infringing materials in China, *Yyets.com* has reportedly shut down at key times, including on or about April 26th, World Intellectual Property Day, and after being nominated for inclusion in this year's List.[26] Visitors to *Yyets.com* currently are redirected to Zimuzu.tv, which appears to offer unauthorized streaming of copyright-protected television programs and movies.

Zing.vn: Vietnam-based Zing.vn, primarily a social media site, reportedly continues to facilitate access to unauthorized music files. Years of negotiations to legitimize its content distribution have still not yielded significant results. Due to the lack of civil and criminal enforcement options against websites in Vietnam, industry filed a copyright infringement case in the United States against Zing.vn's operator, VNG; however, in January 2014, the court dismissed the case on jurisdictional grounds. This highlights the need for

Vietnam to establish effective enforcement mechanisms to address online copyright infringement.

Zippyshare.com: This site is well-known for downloads and distribution of allegedly infringing music. The site offers features that make piracy more "infringer friendly," including through accelerated downloading. Zippyshare is reportedly operated from Poland and hosted in France. Its revenues reportedly come from paid advertising, which targets the millions of users who download files from the site.

Physical Markets

The Internet has brought about a global revolution in the authorized and unauthorized distribution of films, music, software, video games, and books. In many markets, unauthorized online distribution of, or access to, copyright-protected content largely has replaced unauthorized distribution via physical media. In other markets, however, physical media (including CDs, DVDs, video game cartridges, and pre-loaded computer hard drives and other storage devices) continue to be prevalent, with widespread distribution, at times involving local manufacture, through markets such as those identified below.

The Internet also makes available innumerable sites that facilitate the distribution of counterfeit products to consumers worldwide. The volume of individually consigned shipments of counterfeit merchandise from the country of origin to the global community of consumers is growing.[27] However, Internet connectivity and broadband limitations, costs and other obstacles related to shipping and postal delivery, as well as customs and other regulatory controls, often serve as barriers to e-commerce, regardless of whether the merchandise is authorized or counterfeit. Consequently, physical markets, such as the ones listed below, remain the primary distribution channels for pirated and counterfeit goods and services in much of the world.

In response to the 2014 *Federal Register Request*, USTR received fewer nominations for physical markets than in the past. However, several of the nominations identified China as the primary source of counterfeit products. Worldwide, from the Americas, to Africa, to Eastern Europe, and in Southeast Asia, Chinese-origin counterfeit goods find their way into markets, businesses, and homes. In some cases, parties with ties to China manage the wholesale and retail distribution channels that facilitate the flow of counterfeit merchandise, including to markets such as Prado, Italy; Lagos, Nigeria; Ciudad del Este, Paraguay; and Bangkok, Thailand.

In a global environment, enforcement against unscrupulous retailers, although important, will not be sufficient to reduce the flow of counterfeit products. The importance of effective border controls to prevent exportation of counterfeit goods from their countries of manufacture, to prevent importation into the destination country, and to prevent such goods from transiting third countries on their way to destination countries cannot be overstated. Another key to reducing piracy and counterfeiting, however, lies in the ability to influence demand and redirect the consumers who knowingly participate in illicit trade to legitimate alternatives.

Argentina

La Salada (Buenos Aires) continues to operate as South America's largest black market. Sellers of counterfeit and pirated products deal openly because enforcement reportedly has been small-scale and intermittent, at best. Despite appeals by both the United States government and the European Commission to address counterfeiting and piracy in La Salada, the Government of Argentina reportedly tolerates the sale of contraband at the market.[28] Press reports indicate that the market's owners now operate a companion online market, *LaSalada.com.*

Brazil

Galeria Page (Sao Paulo) and the surrounding 25 de Marco Area, Sao Paulo's largest market for counterfeit goods, has reportedly seen an increase in illicit commerce. Sao Paulo's "City Free of Piracy" project was heralded for the positive impact it had locally and throughout Brazil, but a 2013 change in city leadership brought about a shift in focus away from IPR enforcement. The authorities reportedly have conducted some raids against street vendors in the area; however, counterfeiting and piracy appear to be thriving inside and around the buildings at Galeria Page. While USTR acknowledges the efforts of law enforcement agencies and the fiscal environment that may have precipitated the shift in focus, we urge political support for resuming enforcement in and around this flagship market.

China

Physical markets in China continue to facilitate the distribution of significant quantities of counterfeit merchandise for consumption in China and abroad. Some of these markets are well-known, and according to reports, offer an extensive catalogue of products, and will arrange for on-demand manufacture and worldwide shipping of counterfeit products. Some markets have adopted policies and procedures intended to address the availability of counterfeit merchandise, but these are not vigorously enforced by the markets. At the same time, a number of online markets in China have been the subject of deterrent enforcement actions in China's courts, and in many cases Chinese authorities do engage in routine enforcement actions in physical markets as well. The United States welcomes these efforts and recommends their expansion to combat more effectively the scale of the reported problem both in China and worldwide.

The following Chinese markets are key contributors to counterfeiting: According to reports, *Jin Long Pan Foreign Trade Garment Market (Guangzhou)*, wholesales low-quality, relatively inexpensive counterfeit versions of American and other branded apparel and footwear for export to Africa and the Middle East, in particular.

Counterfeit products, predominantly apparel, footwear, and fashion accessories, including sunglasses, perfumes, and handbags, reportedly continue to dominate the offerings at *Jinshun Garment Market (Guangzhou)*. Recent reports indicate that nearly every shop sells exclusively counterfeit goods.

The *Qi Pu Market (Shanghai)* is a wholesale clothing market, housed in five seven-story buildings, offering a wide array of apparel and accessories. Many sellers reportedly conceal their counterfeit products from plain sight. Upon request, customers are reportedly escorted to locations within the market where finished counterfeit products are available for examination and purchase, including in commercial quantities for export.

Many retail vendors at the *Silk Market (Beijing)* reportedly distribute counterfeit consumer and industrial products to Chinese and foreign buyers. Illicit activities reportedly continue at the Silk Market despite welcome efforts by Chinese authorities to work with management and engage in enforcement actions, and even though some rights holders have successfully sued the market's operators. Vendors at the Silk Market reportedly have access to a supply of newly-manufactured counterfeit products to replace those that have been confiscated, and their profits appear to far exceed financial penalties that have been imposed on them. It appears that past civil and administrative enforcement efforts, although imposing some costs, have not actually ended infringement.

All of the shops at *Zengcheng International Jeans Market (Zengcheng)* reportedly represent factories and sell to retail and wholesale clients in China and worldwide, particularly in Africa. Most shops at the market also claim to sell counterfeit merchandise on *Taobao.com.*

Ecuador

Pirated DVDs, CDs, and software, clothing with counterfeit logos, and counterfeit electronic items remain widely available for sale in *La Bahia Market (Guayaquil)*. The occasional administrative enforcement efforts that occur at the market focus mainly on protecting domestic IPR, and are insufficient to address the overall problem. The current absence of criminal penalties for counterfeiting and piracy makes Ecuador an attractive host for organized criminal activity.

India

Numerous markets in India have appeared in past Lists, with no identified meaningful, effective response by the Indian government. The United States continues to raise the importance of IPR protection and enforcement with India, underscoring the need to combat counterfeiting and piracy in both online and physical markets. The United States encourages India to take sustained and coordinated enforcement action at the *Nehru Place (New Delhi)*, previously-listed markets, and numerous other non-listed markets in its territory.

Indonesia

Harco Glodok (Jakarta) is Indonesia's largest trade center for consumer electronics and related goods. This market reportedly also serves as the retail distribution point for a complex piracy and counterfeiting network. The Government of Indonesia's efforts over the past few years have failed to rid this otherwise legitimate market of IPR-infringing goods and services. USTR urges the Indonesian Government to launch a sustained, coordinated, and effective effort to tackle widespread counterfeiting and piracy at Harco Glodok and elsewhere.[29]

Mexico

In the 2014 Notorious Markets process, Mexico ranked first in terms of number of nominated markets. Although several rights holders commented positively on the IPR enforcement efforts of Mexican authorities at the *Tepito (Mexico City)* and *San Juan de Dios (Guadalajara)* markets, significant levels of piracy and counterfeiting reportedly continue in these, and reportedly in dozens of other markets across Mexico. The United States encourages Mexico to continue coordinated law enforcement efforts, including against high-level targets in the distribution chain, to reduce the availability of counterfeit and pirated product in markets across the country. We further encourage Mexico to empower customs officials to interdict infringing imports on their own authority as well to enforce against counterfeit and pirated goods moving in-transit.

Nigeria

The situation in Nigeria exemplifies why both effective import controls at the destination market and export controls at the country of origin are essential in stopping the flow of counterfeit and pirated goods. Nigerian authorities face challenges in allocating sufficient resources and building the necessary infrastructure to engage in effective import controls against the tide of foreign-manufactured counterfeit products. In addition, Nigeria-based piracy operations that target both foreign and Nigerian films and music present challenges for authorities.

Computer Village Market (Ikeja, Lagos State) is known to be the largest market for knockoff computer products and accessories in Nigeria. Raids by regulators continue, but up to an estimated 80 percent of the wide variety of electronic devices, music, movies, and other products available here are counterfeit or pirated. Store owners reportedly cooperate with each other to frustrate or prevent enforcement activities. Enforcement in this market is considered dangerous.

Counterfeit and substandard household items and appliances, are available in the *Ebutte Ero Market (Lagos Island, Lagos State).* IPR enforcement here is not a priority for resource-challenged regulators. The market has been described as tightly organized and difficult to monitor, and enforcement would be a challenge even if resources were available. Stopping counterfeit goods at borders, before they reach the retail distribution level, may be an effective way to address markets such as this.

Sale of counterfeit soft drinks, spirits and popular consumer goods is prevalent in the *Oke-Arin & Apongbon Markets (Lagos Island, Lagos State).* Regulatory agencies have conducted raids and made some arrests, but the chaotic nature of this densely populated market makes enforcement difficult.

Paraguay

Ciudad del Este, Paraguay has been named in either the List or the Special 301 Report for over 15 years. Regional organized crime groups are reportedly trafficking in counterfeit and copyright-infringing goods in Ciudad del Este. The border crossing at Ciudad del Este and the city itself reportedly have served as a hub for the distribution of counterfeit and pirated products in the Brazil-Argentina-Paraguay triple frontier region and beyond. During the past 18 months, the Cartes Administration, primarily through the National Directorate of Intellectual Property (DINAPI), General Enforcement Directorate and partner law enforcement agencies, has engaged in several enforcement efforts. The United States applauds the Cartes Administration's goal of transforming Ciudad del Este into a legitimate marketplace, with all its attendant benefits. While Paraguay's recent efforts merit acknowledgement, years of relative inattention have created a situation in Ciudad del Este that will require further coordinated and sustained enforcement efforts to resolve.

Thailand

IPR holders face a difficult environment in Thailand due to the large number of markets offering counterfeit and pirated goods and services, and a relative lack of enforcement. Last year, USTR identified 13 Thai markets in the List. We appreciate the Government of Thailand's efforts over the past year and for the enforcement statistics it provided in response to the *Federal Register Request*. However, reports indicate that pervasive counterfeiting and piracy continue in all of the previously-listed markets, including at *Talad Nat on Wireless Road (Bangkok)*, near the U.S. Embassy. USTR requests that Thai authorities conduct sustained, coordinated enforcement actions at the "Red Zone" markets listed in last year's report, or at any nominated markets in which counterfeiting and piracy are rampant. USTR will continue to monitor the situation.

Uruguay

Despite Uruguay's otherwise positive reputation for respecting IPR, there has been an increase in reports of counterfeiting and piracy in its *Free Trade Zones* ("FTZs"), including *Florida Sur* and *Libertad.*[30] USTR encourages the Government of Uruguay to work with rights holders to address concerns regarding counterfeit goods, including footwear and apparel, being trafficked in its FTZs. USTR will continue to engage with Uruguay on this issue.

Public Information

The 2014 Notorious Markets List is the result of the fifth OCR of Notorious Markets, which was initiated on September 26, 2014, through a *Federal Register Request for Public Comments*. The request and responses are available at *www.federalregister.gov*, Docket Number USTR-2014- 0017. USTR developed the 2014 List in coordination with the Federal agencies represented on the Special 301 Subcommittee of the Trade Policy Staff Committee (TPSC). Information about Special 301, the TPSC, and other intellectual property rights-related processes and issues is available at *https://ustr.gov/issue-areas/intellectual-property*.

To assist U.S. rights holders and consumers who confront IPR infringement online, the U.S. Government continues to expand the tools available on *www.STOPfakes.gov*, including by providing links to infringement reporting mechanisms at a number of popular online retailers and markets. These resources are available at *www.STOPfakes.gov/business-tools/retailerreporting*. Victims and interested parties may report IPR theft to U.S. law enforcement agencies either through a link at *www.STOPfakes.gov* or directly at *www.iprcenter.gov/referral*.

End Notes

[1] The terms "copyright piracy" and "trademark counterfeiting" appear below as "piracy" and "counterfeiting," respectively.

[2] Please refer to the Public Information section below for links to information and resources related to Special 301.

[3] Previously- and presently-listed markets appear in bold type. When a paragraph includes multiple references to a market only the first instance will appear in bold type.

[4] On January 1, 2015, Spain's new copyright law came into force. The law provides, among other things, significant penalties for unauthorized distribution of copyright-protected content. Reportedly in anticipation of the effective date of the law, several sites popular in Spain either reduced the availability of pirated content or ceased operations. This welcome response will create more opportunities for legitimate content distribution in Spain.

[5] Because Share-rapid.cz may have resumed operations as MegaRapid.cz, USTR will continue to monitor the new site for potential IPR infringement.

[6] Vigilance by Swedish and other government authorities is needed to prevent The Pirate Bay ("TPB") from resuming full operations as it did after a 2006 enforcement action against it. Shortly after the December 2014 enforcement action, the site resumed operations as ThePirateBay.si and then again as ThePirateBay.se as well as under several other domain names. TPB also has been cloned (i.e., substantially identical sites made available under other domain names), including by the operators of Isohunt.to, who also cloned previously-listed Isohunt.com. TPB and several clone sites are reportedly using CloudFlare.com's services.

[7] Boerse.bz, like TPB, appears to have resumed operations, as Boerse.to. The resurgence of sites after enforcement actions reinforces the need for not only coordinated but also sustained responses.

[8] Alexa.com utilizes a proprietary methodology to analyze global and country-specific user traffic and develop a numerical rank that indicates a website's popularity relative to other sites. Rankings can change dramatically and quickly. The rankings that appear in this document are current as of March 3, 2015.

[9] Outils opérationnels de prévention et de lutte contre la contrefaçon en ligne is available at www.culturecommunication.gouv.fr/Ressources/Rapports/Outils-operationnels-de-prevention-et-de-lutte-contre-lacontrefacon-en-ligne. (English language summary: http://merlin.obs.coe.int/iris/2014/6/article18.en.html). Please also see the 2013 Report on the Prevention of Unlawful Streaming and Direct Downloading at http://hadopi.fr/sites/default/files/page/pdf/Rapportstreaming_eng.pdf.

[10] Known as "RogueBlock," this payment processor initiative is a "a collaborative effort of the IACC and the payment industry to create a streamlined, simplified procedure for members to report online sellers of counterfeit or pirated goods directly to credit card and payment processing networks." www.iacc.org/rogueblock.html.

[11] For a discussion of domestic initiatives in selected countries, please see the U.K. Intellectual Property Office's February 2015 publication International Comparison of Approaches to Online Copyright Infringement: Final Report, available at www.gov.uk/government/uploads/system/uploads/attachment_data/file/404429/International_Comparison_of_Appr oaches_to_Online_Copyright_Infringement.pdf.

[12] Access to legitimate alternatives is critical in combatting online piracy. Many governments and rights holders have focused on developing and helping consumers identify legitimate alternatives, for example: www.wheretowatch.com; www.educause.edu/focus-areas-and-initiatives/policy-and-security/educausepolicy/issues-and-positions/intellectual-property /legal-sources-onli; ww.Findanyfilm.com; www.Canistream.it; www.mesientodecine.com; and www.culturaenpositivo.mecd.gob/es.

[13] The SAIC report is no longer available on the SAIC website. According to unofficial translations of the report (see, e.g., http://money.163.com/15/0129/ 13/AH4N7AA K00254TFQ.html), SAIC faulted Alibaba Group for failing to take effective measures to address a range of problems, including against trademark infringement, for requiring parties to waive claims to operator liability, and for imposing unreasonable burdens on consumers who wish to file complaints.

[14] According to Bulgarian officials, inspectors cut access to over 20,000 files of illegal content on zamunda.net, zamunda.se, arenabg.com and another peer-to-peer site, VBox7, in 2014.

[15] For information on ICANN's policies and procedures, please visit www.stopfakes.gov/news/protectingtrademarks-domain-names; and www.icann.org/resources/pages/ compla ints-2013-03-22-en.

[16] ICANN's Registrar Accreditation Agreements are available at www.icann.org/resources/pages/approved-withspecs-2013-09-17-en; and www.icann.org/resources/pages/ra-agreement-2009-05-21-en.

[17] The Alliance for Safe Online Pharmacies' ("ASOP") filing referenced LegitScript.com, a pharmacist-affiliated online pharmacy verification authority, that also publishes lists of reportedly illicit online drug sellers and unresponsive domain name registrars. ASOP nominated for inclusion in the 2014 List several of the same registrars identified by LegitScript. For details on the selection process and the current registrar and pharmacy lists as well as other important information regarding online pharmacies, please visit: http://www.legitscript.com/pharmacies/toprogues; and https://blog.legitscript.com/2014/10/top-10-rogue-registrars-october-2014. Additional consumer information regarding online pharmacies can be found at the following websites: http://safeonlinerx.com; www.safemed sonline.org; and www.nabp.net/programs/accreditation/vipps. While these sites focus primarily on the U.S. audience, similar resources are available to consumers outside the United States, including at http://asop.eu/home. Related U.S. Government resources and information, including on voluntary initiatives spearheaded by the Executive Office of the

President's U.S. Intellectual Property Enforcement Coordinator, are available at: www.whitehouse.gov/sites/default/files/omb/IPEC/2013-us-ipec-joint-strategic-plan.pdf (page 35); and www.fda.gov/Drugs/ResourcesForYou/ucm080588.htm.

[18] National Association of Boards of Pharmacy (NABP), http//safeonlinerx.com/wp-content/uploads/2012/07/nabpinternet-drug-outlet-identification-program-report_apr2010.pdf) (page 4). This report includes troubling statistics regarding over 5,000 online drug outlets "Not Recommended" by the NABP as trustworthy sources of pharmaceutical products. Please also see the U.S. Government Accountability Office Report on Internet Pharmacies at www.gao.gov/assets/660/655751.pdf.

[19] World Health Organization, www.who.int/mediacentre/factsheets/fs275/en.

[20] Interpol, www.interpol.int/en/Crime-areas/Pharmaceutical-crime/The-dangers.

[21] Increasingly, operators of online notorious markets are using Country Code Top Level Domains ("ccTLDs"), which are subject to greater government influence, rather than generic or gTLDs. Governments are strongly encouraged to take an active role in preventing the use of their ccTLDs to facilitate the sale and distribution of counterfeit and pirated products and services.

[22] In most cases, the List identifies online markets by the domain name provided in the public responses to the Federal Register Request. However, it is common for operators of online Notorious Markets to change a site's domain name or to use multiple domain names at once to direct users to the main site. The List reflects each market's most commonly referred to or well-known domain name or names as of March 3, 2015.

[23] The cyberlockers identified in the List reportedly operate primarily to provide users with access to unauthorized content. Such sites are distinguishable from legitimate cloud storage services that allow consumers to lawfully store, share, backup, and access data. For more information on cyberlockers' role in facilitating piracy, please see www.netnames.com/sites/default/files/pdfs/dca-netnames-cyber-profibility.pdf.

[24] USTR received information regarding Canadian online pharmacies in response to our Federal Register 2015 Special 301 Request for Public Comments. For more information, please refer to www.federalregister.gov, Docket Number USTR-2014-0025.

[25] Although Bizcn.com (also operating as Cndomainsite.com) was also nominated for inclusion in the List based on concerns similar to those reported for Tucows, it appears that the operator of Bixcn.com has recently undertaken efforts to address these serious problems. USTR welcomes this apparent positive development but urges Bizcn to sustain and expand this important effort.

[26] Chinese administrative authorities have issued penalties against Yyets.com and other online markets.

[27] For example, the European Union recently enhanced its border enforcement authority to address the increase in trafficking of counterfeit goods via small, postal or express courier consignments. Please see http://eurlex.europa.eu/legal-content/EN/TXT/?uri=CELEX:52005DC0479.

[28] Representatives of La Salada reportedly accompanied the President of Argentina on trade missions abroad. Past administrations have also appeared to tolerate the counterfeiting and piracy at La Salada. Please see www.economist.com/news/americas/21594998-inside-south-americas-largest-informal-market-stall-stories.

[29] Other markets in Indonesia, including those named in previous Lists, were not identified in response to this year's Federal Register Request, but nonetheless require attention.

[30] Information on the general challenge of enforcing IPR in FTZs is available at www.iccwbo.org/Advocacy-Codesand-Rules/BASCAP/International-engagement-and-Advocacy/Free-Trade-Zones.

In: International Approaches ...
Editor: Patricia Wade
ISBN: 978-1-63483-168-0

Chapter 3

SAFE HARBOR FOR ONLINE SERVICE PROVIDERS UNDER SECTION 512(C) OF THE DIGITAL MILLENNIUM COPYRIGHT ACT*

Brian T. Yeh

SUMMARY

Congress passed the Digital Millennium Copyright Act (DMCA) in 1998 in an effort to adapt copyright law to emerging digital technologies that potentially could be used to exponentially increase infringing activities online. Title II of the DMCA, titled the "Online Copyright Infringement Liability Limitation Act," added a new Section 512 to the Copyright Act (Title 17 of the U.S. Code) in order to limit the liability of providers of Internet access and online services that may arise due to their users posting or sharing materials that infringe copyrights. Congress was concerned that without insulating Internet intermediaries from crippling financial liability for copyright infringement, investment in the growth of the Internet could be stifled and innovation could be harmed.

The § 512 "safe harbor" immunity is available only to a party that qualifies as a "service provider" as defined by the DMCA, and only after the provider complies with certain eligibility requirements. The DMCA's safe harbors greatly limit service providers' liability based on the specific functions they could perform: (1) transitory digital network

* This is an edited, reformatted and augmented version of a Congressional Research Service publication, No. R43436, dated March 26, 2014.

communications, (2) system caching, (3) storage of information on systems or networks at direction of users, and (4) information location tools. In exchange for the shelter from most forms of liability, the DMCA requires service providers to cooperate with copyright owners to address infringing activities conducted by the providers' customers. The safe harbor thus reflects a "grand bargain" between creative content-producing industries and Internet companies that seeks to both promote investment in the Internet and protect copyright holders' intellectual property rights.

The DMCA expressly states that a service provider is not required to actively monitor its service for infringing activity. However, § 512 requires a service provider, upon proper notification by the copyright owner of online material being displayed or transmitted without authorization, to "expeditiously" remove or disable access to the allegedly infringing material. In addition, a service provider must remove or disable access to material upon acquiring actual knowledge that materials or activities on its system or network are infringing (for example, actual knowledge can be obtained by the copyright holder's notification) *or* when the service provider becomes aware of facts or circumstances from which infringing activity is apparent (so-called "red flag" knowledge). Service providers that meet the eligibility conditions of the § 512 safe harbor are thus shielded from liability for *unknowingly* hosting content that infringes copyrights, whereas § 512 provides copyright holders a simple and cost-effective procedural mechanism for remedying online infringement of their intellectual property rights. Courts have found that the burden of actively monitoring online copyright infringement lies on copyright holders.

This report focuses primarily on the third safe harbor functional category, "storage of information on systems or networks at direction of users," which includes any website that stores digital content that users have uploaded for public consumption or for sharing purposes, such as popular social media and online services YouTube, Facebook, Dropbox, Flickr, Google Drive, and Blogger. The report will describe and analyze the statutory language establishing the safe harbor as well as discuss federal court cases that have considered the scope and application of the DMCA safe harbors and the extent to which online service providers can be held indirectly liable for copyright infringement committed by their users.

INTRODUCTION

Online service providers (OSPs) and Internet service providers (ISPs) provide critical infrastructure support to the Internet, allowing millions of people to access online content and electronically communicate and interact with each other. The potential for computer users to infringe intellectual property rights using the Internet, specifically copyrights, could expose "intermediary" service providers to claims of secondary liability, such as contributory and vicarious copyright infringement. Concerned about this significant legal vulnerability of service providers, Congress passed the "Online Copyright Infringement Liability Limitation Act," Title II of the Digital Millennium Copyright Act (DMCA) of 1998,[1] in an effort to adapt copyright law to an evolving digital environment.[2] The act added a new Section 512 to the Copyright Act (Title 17 of the U.S. Code), which provides limitations on the liability of OSPs and ISPs against claims of copyright infringement arising from their users' activities on their digital networks.[3]

The act's legislative history indicates that Congress wanted to provide service providers with "more certainty ... in order to attract the substantial investments necessary to continue the expansion and upgrading of the Internet."[4] At the same time, Congress desired to preserve "strong incentives for service providers and copyright owners to cooperate to detect and deal with copyright infringements that take place in the digital networked environment."[5] The DMCA therefore includes several conditions that the service provider must satisfy in order to qualify for § 512 "safe harbor" protection from most infringement liability, and requires that the service providers' activities be encompassed within one of four specified categories of conduct. The safe harbors correspond to the following four functional operations that might otherwise constitute copyright infringement: (1) transitory digital network communications, (2) system caching, (3) storage of information on systems or networks at direction of users, and (4) information location tools.[6]

One federal district court assessed the "dual purpose and balance" of § 512 in the following manner:

> Congress created tradeoffs within the DMCA: service providers would receive liability protections in exchange for assisting copyright owners in identifying and dealing with infringers who misuse the service providers' systems. At the same time, copyright owners would forgo pursuing service providers for the copyright infringement of their users, in exchange for assistance in identifying and acting against those infringers.[7]

A public interest group has praised the importance of the DMCA's safe harbor provisions to the development of the Internet:

> Without these protections, the risk of potential copyright liability would prevent many online intermediaries from providing services such as hosting and transmitting user-generated content. Thus the safe harbors have been essential to the growth of the Internet as an engine for innovation and free expression.[8]

Although all four safe harbors will be described at the beginning of this report, the primary focus for the rest of the report will be on the third category that encompasses the function of many popular Internet businesses today: "storage of information on systems or networks at direction of users." This safe harbor is essential to the business model of most ISPs and OSPs that permit user generated content (UGC) to be stored or shared using their networks.

BACKGROUND

Copyright is a federal grant of legal protection available to the creator or owner of certain original works of creative expression, including books, movies, photography, art, and music.[9] A copyright holder possesses several exclusive legal entitlements under the Copyright Act, which together provide the holder with the right to determine whether and under what circumstances the protected work may be used by third parties. The grant of copyright permits the copyright holder to authorize or refuse to authorize others to exercise the following exclusive rights:

- the reproduction of the copyrighted work;
- the preparation of derivative works based on the copyrighted work;
- the distribution of copies of the copyrighted work;
- the public performance of the copyrighted work; and
- the public display of the copyrighted work, including the individual images of a motion picture.[10]

Therefore, a party desiring to reproduce, adapt, distribute, publicly display, or publicly perform a copyrighted work must either (1) obtain the permission of the copyright holder (usually granted in the form of a license agreement that establishes conditions of use and an amount of monetary compensation known as a royalty fee); (2) comply with the terms of compulsory licenses established by law;[11] or (3) assert that such use falls within the scope of certain statutory limitations on the exclusive rights such as the "fair use" doctrine—but the validity of such claim may be subject to the judgment of a federal court.[12]

Each exclusive right of a copyright holder is potentially subject to licensing; for example, a third party wishing to reproduce a copyrighted work as well as publicly perform the work must negotiate separate licenses from the copyright holder to engage in the different activities.

Unauthorized use of a copyrighted work by a third party in a manner that implicates one of the copyright holder's exclusive rights constitutes infringement.[13] The copyright holder may file a lawsuit in federal court against an alleged infringer for a violation of any of the exclusive rights conferred by copyright. The Copyright Act provides several civil remedies to the copyright holder that is harmed by infringement, including the possibility of obtaining injunctive relief,[14] actual damages suffered by the copyright owner due to the infringement,[15] statutory damages,[16] and costs and attorney fees.[17]

The rights conferred by a copyright do not last forever. Copyrights are limited in the number of years a copyright holder may exercise his/her exclusive rights. In general, an author of a creative work may enjoy copyright protection for the work for a term lasting the entirety of his/her life plus 70 additional years.[18] At the expiration of a term, the copyrighted work becomes part of the public domain. A work in the public domain is available for anyone to use without the need to seek prior permission of the creator of the work.

Secondary Liability for Copyright Infringement

Someone who *directly* infringes a copyright is not the only party potentially liable for infringement; one who significantly "aids and abets" another party's commission of a direct infringement may also be sued by the rights holder for *indirect*, or secondary, infringement. The concept of secondary infringement has its roots in tort law and the notion that one should be held accountable for directly contributing to another's infringement.[19] The federal courts have recognized secondary infringement liability in copyright and trademark law, while the Patent Act contains provisions that expressly authorize it.[20] Because online service providers often solely provide the means for their users to upload and distribute content, rather than providing the content themselves, service providers are more likely to be charged with secondary infringement liability rather than sued for direct infringement.

In copyright law, there are three common theories of indirect infringement liability: contributory, vicarious, and inducement liability. For contributory copyright infringement liability to exist, a court must find that the secondary infringer "with knowledge of the infringing activity, induces, causes or materially contributes to the infringing conduct of another."[21] "Vicarious" infringement liability in copyright law is possible where a defendant "has the right and ability to supervise the infringing activity and also has a direct financial interest in such activities."[22] In 2005, the U.S. Supreme Court expressly adopted a relatively new theory of secondary infringement in copyright cases referred to as "inducement liability." In *Metro-Goldwyn-Mayer Studios, Inc. v. Grokster, Ltd.,* the Court articulated the standard for inducement liability:

> [O]ne who distributes a device with the object of promoting its use to infringe copyright, as shown by clear expression or other affirmative steps taken to foster infringement, is liable for the resulting acts of infringement by third parties. ... [M]ere knowledge of infringing potential or of actual infringing uses would not be enough here to subject a distributor to liability. ... The inducement rule, instead, premises liability on purposeful, culpable expression and conduct... [23]

User Generated Content and the Internet

Copyright protection extends to electronic documents, videos, photos, music, and other copyrightable subject matter that may be accessible via the Internet. Uploading and downloading copyrighted works without the authorization of the copyright holders is generally a violation of the copyright holders' exclusive rights to control, respectively, the distribution and reproduction of their works.[24] However, the fair use doctrine may apply to materials that are posted on websites—that is, someone accused of online copyright infringement may be able to assert fair use to escape liability; as explained above, however, a federal court would need to determine whether the use of such material on a website qualifies as a fair use.

Several types of Internet technologies enable the storage and sharing of "user generated content" (UGC), which is digital content (such as documents, photographs, music, and video) that is supplied by Internet end-users. Many Internet businesses rely on their users to upload and share UGC to further interest in and usage of their websites or software. In most cases, the UGC is protected by copyright (whether owned by the user or a third party), although online posting or sharing of the material may be authorized by the copyright holder (for promotional purposes, for example), the copyright holder may not object to the posting, or the particular unauthorized activity could nevertheless qualify for a liability defense such as "fair use."

A commonly used UGC technology is the "cyberlocker" or "file hosting service," which provides online storage in the Internet "cloud" for users' digital files. After users have uploaded their files to the online storage location, they may access them from mobile devices or other computers as well as share them publicly or with designated friends and coworkers. Dropbox, Google Drive, YouTube, Facebook, and Instagram are all examples of such cyberlocker services. Although these services all require their users to agree to "Terms of Use" or "Terms of Service" that specifically prohibit the uploading of copyrighted content which they do not have the legal right to post, users often violate these terms by engaging in the unauthorized uploading and sharing of copyrighted music files, television shows, and movies.

SAFE HARBOR PROVISIONS

Limitations on liability, often called "safe harbors," shelter service providers from copyright infringement suits. The DMCA's safe harbor provisions, codified at 17 U.S.C. § 512, do not confer absolute immunity, but they do significantly limit service providers' liability based on the specific functions they perform.[25] The safe harbors correspond to four functional operations of a service provider: (1) transitory digital network communications, (2) system caching, (3) storage of information on systems or networks at direction of users, and (4) information location tools.[26]

Eligibility Threshold for Any Safe Harbor

For protection under any of the safe harbor provisions, a party must first meet the statutory definition of a "service provider." The DMCA provides two distinct definitions, one applicable to the first safe harbor category and the second applicable to all of the others. Under § 512(a), the transitory communications provision, "service provider" is narrowly defined as "an entity offering the transmission, routing, or providing of connections for digital online communications, between or among points specified by a user, of material of the user's choosing, without modification to the content of the material as sent or received."[27] The remaining three subsections utilize a broader definition of "service provider," applicable to "a provider of online services or network access, or the operator of facilities therefor."[28] For example, this definition encompasses providers offering "Internet access, e-mail, chat room and web page hosting services."[29]

After a party qualifies as a service provider under one of the applicable definitions, there are still two additional threshold requirements that the provider must satisfy:[30]

- The service provider must have adopted, reasonably implemented, and informed its users of a "repeat infringer" policy for the termination of the accounts of subscribers who are repeat copyright infringers.
- The provider must accommodate, and not interfere with, "standard technical measures"[31] that are used by copyright owners to identify or protect their works, such as digital watermarks on photographs or digital rights management technologies embedded in videos.

In addition to the three threshold criteria listed above, a service provider must satisfy the specific requirements of the particular safe harbor in question, which are described in the section below.

Note that qualification for any one of these safe harbors is limited to the criteria detailed in each safe harbor provision, and qualification under one safe harbor category does not affect the eligibility determination for any of the other three.[32]

Requirements for Each Safe Harbor

§ 512(a) Transitory Digital Network Communications

When a service provider acts as a data conduit at the request of a third party by "transmitting, routing, or providing connections for, material through a system or network controlled or operated by or for the service provider," it will be shielded from liability for copyright infringement.[33] This safe harbor also protects the service provider for any intermediate and transient storage of the material in the course of conveying the digital information. However, qualification for this safe harbor is subject to several conditions, including the following:[34]

- Data transmission occurs through an automated technical process without selection of the material by the service provider.
- The service provider does not determine the recipients of the material.
- Intermediate or transient copies stored on the provider's system or network must not be accessible to anyone other than the designated recipients, and such copies must not be retained on the system longer than is reasonably necessary.
- The provider must not have modified the content of the transmitted material.

§ 512(b) System Caching

The second safe harbor category limits ISP liability when it engages in "caching" of online content for purposes of improving network performance. Caching[35] helps to reduce the service provider's network congestion and increase download speeds for subsequent requests for the same data. For example, subscribers to a service provider may transmit certain material to other users of the provider's system or network, at the direction of those users. The service provider may, via an automated process, retain copies of this material for a limited time "so that subsequent requests for the same material can be fulfilled by transmitting the retained copy, rather than retrieving the material from the original source on the network."[36] Immunity for service providers that utilize system caching is provided on the condition that the ISP complies with the following:[37]

- The content of cached material that is transmitted to subsequent users is not modified by the service provider.
- The provider complies with industry standard rules regarding the refreshing, reloading, or other updating of the cached material.
- The provider does not interfere with the ability of technology that returns "hit" count information that would otherwise have been collected had the website not been cached to the person who posted the material.
- The provider must impose the same conditions that the original poster of the material required for access, such as passwords or payment of a fee.
- The provider must remove or block access to any material that is posted without the copyright owner's authorization, upon being notified that such material has been previously removed from the originating site, or that the copyright owner has obtained a court order

for the material to be removed from the originating site or to have access to the material be disabled.

§ 512(c) Information Residing on Systems or Networks at Direction of Users

This safe harbor, which is the primary focus of this report, protects against copyright infringement claims due to storage of infringing material at the direction of a user on ISP systems or networks. Such storage includes "providing server space for a user's website, for a chat room, or other forum in which material may be posted at the direction of users."[38] The conditions placed on receiving the benefit of this safe harbor are as follows:[39]

- The service provider lacks actual knowledge of the infringing material hosted or posted on its system or network.
- In the absence of actual knowledge, the service provider is "not aware of facts or circumstances from which infringing activity is apparent."[40]
- Upon obtaining either actual knowledge or awareness of infringing material, the service provider must "act[] expeditiously to remove, or disable access to, the material."[41]
- Where the provider has the right and ability to control the infringing activity, it must not derive a financial benefit directly attributable to that activity.
- Upon receiving proper notification of claimed infringement, the service provider must act "expeditiously" to remove or block access to the material.
- The service provider must designate an agent to receive notifications of claimed infringement. The contact information for this agent must be filed with the Register of Copyrights[42] and also be displayed to the public on the service provider's website.
- Copyright owners must adhere to a prescribed procedure to inform the provider's designated agent of claimed infringement. To constitute effective notification, the copyright owner must "comply substantially" with the statutory requirements of § 512(c)(3):[43]
    1) The notification is in writing, signed physically or electronically by a person authorized to act on behalf of the owner of the copyright allegedly infringed.

2) The notification identifies the material that is claimed to have been infringed and provides sufficient information allowing the service provider to locate the material.
3) The complaining party includes a statement, under penalty of perjury, that the party has a "good faith belief" that the use of the material is not authorized by the copyright owner, and that the information in the notification is accurate.

§ 512(d) Information Location Tools

The fourth safe harbor classification immunizes service providers that provide users access to websites that contain infringing material by using "information location tools" such as hypertext links, indexes, and directories.[44] The conditions attached are substantially similar to those that apply to the "system storage" safe harbor provision discussed above, § 512(c), including lack of actual or constructive knowledge requirements, notice and take-down procedures, and absence of direct financial benefit.[45] The rationale for protecting service providers under this provision is to promote development of the search tools that make finding information possible on the Internet.[46] Without a safe harbor for providers of these tools, the human editors and cataloguers compiling Internet directories might be overly cautious for fear of being held liable for infringement.

Takedown Notices

One condition common to three of the four categories is the requirement that upon proper notification by the copyright owner of online material being displayed or transmitted without authorization, a service provider must "expeditiously" remove or disable access to the allegedly infringing material.[47] This "notice and takedown" obligation does not apply when the service provider functions as a passive conduit of information under § 512(a), but is a condition that must be met to obtain shelter under the remaining three safe harbor provisions. As indicated by the eligibility conditions in each subsection of § 512(b)-(d), the notice and takedown procedure varies slightly for each.

To prevent abuse of the notice and takedown procedure, § 512(f) provides damages, costs, and attorneys' fees to any service provider that is injured by a knowing, material misrepresentation that an item or activity is infringing.[48] For example, any person who sends a "cease and desist" letter to a service provider, with the knowledge that the claims of copyright infringement are false, may be liable to the accused infringer for damages.

Limited Injunctive Relief Still Possible

As noted earlier, the DMCA's safe harbor provisions do not confer absolute immunity from legal liability for copyright infringement. Although they ensure that qualifying service providers are not liable for monetary damages, service providers may still be liable for certain injunctive relief. For example, in the case of service providers that provide either (1) system caching, (2) storage of information on systems or networks at direction of users, or (3) information location tools, the court may grant injunctive relief with respect to a service provider in one or more of the following forms:

- an order restraining the service provider from providing access to infringing material or activity residing at a particular online site on the provider's system or network;
- an order restraining the service provider from providing access to a subscriber or account holder of the service provider's system or network who is engaging in infringing activity and is identified in the order, by terminating the accounts of the subscriber or account holder that are specified in the order;
- such other injunctive relief as the court may consider necessary to prevent or restrain infringement of copyrighted material specified in the order of the court at a particular online location, if such relief is the least burdensome to the service provider among the forms of relief comparably effective for that purpose.[49]

JUDICIAL INTERPRETATIONS OF THE § 512(C) SAFE HARBOR

Since the enactment of the DMCA, many online service providers have been the target of infringement lawsuits by large companies that own copyrighted content, particularly recorded music, television shows, and motion pictures. These lawsuits typically accuse the service provider of direct, vicarious, and contributory copyright infringement, as well as inducement of infringement. The cases often begin by the service provider asserting a DMCA safe harbor as an affirmative defense that limits its infringement liability; as an affirmative defense, the service provider has the burden of establishing that it meets the safe harbor's eligibility requirements.[50] If this burden is satisfied, courts often find for the defendant on summary judgment. It is important to keep in mind that a service provider's inability to qualify for a safe harbor does not mean that it is presumptively liable for copyright infringement; rather, the copyright holder must still prove its infringement claim.

Through the many cases in which the § 512(c) safe harbor is asserted as protecting a service provider from some forms of infringement liability, the federal courts have had an opportunity to interpret the statutory language and evaluate the scope of the safe harbor's application. What follows is a discussion of these cases.

Burden of Policing Infringement

Section 512(m) expressly provides that the DMCA's safe harbor provisions are not conditioned upon a service provider "monitoring its service or affirmatively seeking facts indicating infringing activity."[51] The federal courts generally agree that the DMCA imposes the duty to police infringement on the copyright holders, not the service providers. In *Perfect 10, Inc. v. CCBill LLC,* the Ninth Circuit Court of Appeals explained that

> The DMCA notification procedures place the burden of policing copyright infringement— identifying the potentially infringing material and adequately documenting infringement— squarely on the owners of the copyright. We decline to shift a substantial burden from the copyright owner to the provider...[52]

The district court in *Viacom International, Inc. v. YouTube, Inc.,* agreed with the *Perfect 10* appellate court, remarking that placing the burden on the copyright holder to monitor for infringing activity

> makes sense, as the infringing works in suit may be a small fraction of millions of works posted by others on the service's platform, whose provider cannot by inspection determine whether the use has been licensed by the owner, or whether its posting is a "fair use" of the material, or even whether its copyright owner or licensee objects to its posting.[53]

Definition of "Storage"

In *Viacom International, Inc. v. YouTube, Inc.*, the large media conglomerate Viacom argued (among many other things) that YouTube, the most popular video-sharing website, did not qualify for the § 512(c) safe harbor because it replicates, transmits, and displays videos, rather than merely "stores" the UGC. The district court disagreed with Viacom's proposed narrow definition of "storage," and explained that the statutory definition of "service provider" is defined as "a provider of online services or network access, or the operator of facilities therefor," and includes "an entity offering the transmission, routing, or providing of connections for digital online communications."[54] Thus, the court held that the "collateral scope" of "storage" includes YouTube's offering of software functions that facilitate user access to the UGC, which include reproduction, display, or performance of the videos.[55]

Repeat Infringer Termination Policy

In *Ellison v. Robertson,*[56] the defendant service provider was denied safe harbor protection for failure to meet the threshold eligibility requirements under § 512(i), the "repeat infringer termination policy" provision. Stephen Robertson had electronically scanned and converted into digital files several science fiction novels written by Harlan Ellison, without authorization of the copyright owner. Robertson then uploaded and copied the files onto newsgroups that are carried by several ISPs, including America Online, Inc. (AOL). Once Ellison learned of the infringing activity, he e-mailed a notice of copyright infringement pursuant to the DMCA notification procedures. AOL, however, claimed never to have received the notice. Receiving no response, the plaintiff then filed a copyright infringement suit against AOL and other parties.

The Ninth Circuit Court of Appeals reversed the district court's conclusion that AOL qualified for a safe harbor limitation of liability. The appellate court found "at least a triable issue of material fact" regarding AOL's threshold eligibility for safe harbor under § 512(i).[57] First, the court explained that § 512(i)(1)(A) has three separate requirements for a service provider to fulfill:

- Adopt a policy that provides for the termination of service access for repeat copyright infringers in appropriate circumstances.
- Inform users of the service policy.
- Implement the policy in a reasonable manner.

The court determined that there was "ample evidence in the record" to suggest that AOL failed to satisfy the last of these requirements. Because AOL had changed the e-mail address to which infringement notifications were being sent and did not close the old e-mail account or forward the messages to the new address, "AOL allowed notices of potential copyright infringement to fall into a vacuum and to go unheeded."[58] This fact alone provides a basis for a reasonable jury to find that AOL did not "reasonably implement[]" a policy against repeat infringers.[59]

Notification Requirement

In *ALS Scan, Inc. v. RemarQ Communities, Inc.*, the Fourth Circuit Court of Appeals considered whether a service provider is eligible for protection when it is alerted to infringing activity by "imperfect notice" that does not strictly comply with the notification procedures specified in § 512(c)(3).[60] ALS Scan holds the copyrights to over 10,000 "adult" photographs which were posted on newsgroups that were operated by the service provider RemarQ Communities. Upon discovering that RemarQ's servers contained infringing material, ALS Scan sent a "cease and desist" letter to RemarQ, requesting deletion of two specific newsgroups that contained the photographs. However, the district court in *ALS Scan* found that the notice was "fatally defective" in complying with § 512(c)(3) because ALS Scan never provided RemarQ with a "representative list" of the infringing photographs. Nor did it identify the pornographic photographs with "sufficient detail" to enable RemarQ to locate and disable access to them.[61] In reversing the district court's ruling granting summary judgment in favor of RemarQ, the court of appeals held that ALS Scan had "substantially complied" with DMCA notification requirements because its notice letter identified by name the two RemarQ newsgroup sites "created solely for the purpose of publishing and exchanging ALS Scan's copyrighted images" and also referred RemarQ to website addresses where RemarQ could find pictures and names of ALS Scan's adult models.[62] Thus, the court of appeals held that since RemarQ was provided with a notice that *substantially* complied with the DMCA, the service provider could not rely on a claim of defective notice to maintain the safe harbor defense.[63]

Actual Knowledge of Infringement

The DMCA requires a service provider to remove or disable access to material upon obtaining "actual knowledge that the material or an activity using the material on the system or network is infringing."[64] (A service provider may also choose to ignore its actual knowledge of infringement, but doing so would render it ineligible for safe harbor protection.) A mere "generalized awareness" of infringement, even if it may be prevalent throughout its digital network or system, does not impose a legal duty on a service provider to monitor or search for infringements.[65] Rather, a service provider must have "knowledge of specific and identifiable infringements of particular individual items" before the legal duty is triggered.[66] The Second Circuit Court of Appeals in *Viacom International, Inc. v. YouTube, Inc.* reasoned that "the nature of the removal obligation itself contemplates knowledge or awareness of specific infringing material, because expeditious removal is possible only if the service provider knows with particularity which items to remove."[67]

In *Corbis Corp. v. Amazon.com, Inc.*,[68] the federal district court determined that the electronic commerce company Amazon.com had qualified for safe harbor with regard to infringing activity allegedly occurring in its zShops third-party vendor service.[69] Corbis, a company that licenses art images and celebrity photographs, had sued Amazon, claiming that several hundred images in which it had a "copyright interest" were being copied, displayed, and sold through Amazon's zShops sites.[70] Amazon sought liability protection under the § 512(c) safe harbor. The court found that Amazon did not have actual knowledge that material on its network is infringing because Corbis, prior to filing the lawsuit, had never attempted to notify Amazon about the alleged infringing conduct of zShop vendors. Thus, the court explained, Corbis missed its opportunity to provide "the most powerful evidence of a service provider's knowledge–actual notice of infringement from the copyright holder."[71]

In *UMG Recordings, Inc. v. Shelter Capital Partners LLC*, Universal Music Group (UMG), one of the largest recorded music and music publishing companies, sued Veoh Networks, an operator of a website that allowed users to share videos with others.[72] First, the Ninth Circuit Court of Appeals observed that UMG had not notified Veoh of any specific infringing video on its system and thus, like Corbis Corporation, the failure to use the formal DMCA notice protocol "stripped it of the most powerful evidence of a service provider's knowledge."[73] UMG argued, however, that Veoh, by hosting a category of copyrighted content such as "music videos" for which it had no license from any major music company, had actual knowledge of the infringing material on its website.[74] The appellate court rejected this proposition, holding that with only the "general knowledge that one's services could be used to share infringing material," a service provider lacks actual knowledge of infringement.[75]

"Red Flag" Apparent Knowledge of Infringement

In the absence of "actual knowledge" that materials or activities on their system or network are infringing, a service provider has an obligation to "expeditiously" remove or disable access to infringing content when it becomes "aware of facts or circumstances from which infringing activity is apparent."[76] The service provider's duty to remove material upon obtaining an "awareness" of apparent infringing activity is the so-called "red flag" provision of the DMCA and it is distinct from the "actual knowledge" requirement discussed in the previous section.

In *Perfect 10 Inc. v. CCBill LLC,* the Ninth Circuit Court of Appeals disagreed with the plaintiff's allegation that the defendants (who provided web hosting services to other websites) had received notice of apparent infringement from "red flags" such as websites that were named "illegal.net" and "stolencelebritypics.com."[77] The appellate court explained that "[w]hen a website traffics in pictures that are titillating by nature, describing photographs as 'illegal' or 'stolen' may be an attempt to increase their salacious appeal, rather than an admission that the photographs are actually illegal or stolen. We do not place the burden of determining whether photographs are actually illegal on a service provider."[78]

The appellate court in *Viacom International, Inc. v. YouTube, Inc.* described the difference between actual knowledge and "red flag knowledge" as being "between a subjective and an objective standard:"

> [T]he actual knowledge provision turns on whether the provider actually or "subjectively" knew of specific infringement, while the red flag provision turns on whether the provider was subjectively

> aware of facts that would have made the specific infringement "objectively" obvious to a reasonable person. The red flag provision, because it incorporates an objective standard, is not swallowed up by the actual knowledge provision under our construction of the § 512(c) safe harbor. Both provisions do independent work, and both apply only to specific instances of infringement.[79]

Willful Blindness

The doctrine of willful blindness is used widely within the federal judiciary in criminal law cases involving criminal statutes that require proof that a defendant acted knowingly or willfully, in order to hold defendants accountable so that they "cannot escape the reach of these statutes by deliberately shielding themselves from clear evidence of critical facts that are strongly suggested by the circumstances."[80] The Supreme Court has previously explained that "persons who know enough to blind themselves to direct proof of critical facts *in effect* have actual knowledge of those facts."[81]

In a case examining induced patent infringement liability, *Global-Tech Appliances, Inc. v. SEB S.A.*,[82] the Supreme Court described a two-part test for the willful blindness doctrine:

1) The defendant must subjectively believe that there is a high probability that a fact exists.
2) The defendant must take deliberate actions to avoid learning of that fact.[83]

The Court believed that these two requirements of the willful blindness doctrine provide "an appropriately limited scope that surpasses recklessness and negligence."[84] The differences between these three standards, according to the Court, are as follows:

- "[A] willfully blind defendant is one who takes deliberate actions to avoid confirming a high probability of wrongdoing and who can almost be said to have actually known the critical facts."
- "[A] reckless defendant is one who merely knows of a substantial and unjustified risk of such wrongdoing."
- "[A] negligent defendant is one who should have known of a similar risk but, in fact, did not."[85]

The Second Circuit Court of Appeals in *Viacom International, Inc. v. YouTube, Inc.* was the first appellate court to consider the application of the common law willful blindness doctrine in the DMCA context. The court acknowledged that the DMCA does not expressly mention willful blindness. Nevertheless, the court held that the doctrine could apply in certain circumstances "to demonstrate knowledge or awareness of specific instances of infringements under the DMCA,"[86] for example, if a service provider makes deliberate efforts to avoid obtaining knowledge of specific infringing activity.

The Ninth Circuit Court of Appeals in *UMG Recordings, Inc. v.* Shelter Capital Partners LLC also agreed with the *Viacom* appellate court that "a service provider cannot willfully bury its head in the sand to avoid obtaining such specific knowledge."[87] However, in the case at hand, the court found "no evidence that Veoh acted in such a manner," but instead noted that "Veoh promptly removed infringing material when it became aware of specific instances of infringement."[88]

"Right and Ability to Control" Infringing Activity

Section 512(c)(1)(B) specifies that for a service provider to be eligible for the safe harbor applicable to online storage functions, the provider must not receive a "financial benefit directly attributable to the infringing activity" that it has the "right and ability to control."[89] The federal courts have held that the ability of a service provider to remove or block access to materials posted on its website or stored on its network is *not enough* to prove that the service provider had the "right and ability to control" the infringing activity.[90] Instead, the courts have required evidence of "something more" than the service provider's technical ability to remove or block infringing materials, which demonstrates the service provider's ability to exert "substantial influence on the activities of users."[91] For example, the federal district court in *Perfect 10, Inc. v. Cybernet Ventures, Inc.* found the requisite control where the service provider had established a monitoring program by which its webmasters received "detailed instructions regard[ing] issues of layout, appearance, and content."[92] The service provider also forbade certain types of content and refused access to users who failed to comply with its instructions. In addition, the appellate court in *Viacom International, Inc. v. YouTube, Inc.* suggested that "inducement of copyright infringement under *Metro-Goldwyn-Mayer Studios Inc. v. Grokster, Ltd.*, which "premises liability on purposeful, culpable expression and conduct," might also rise to the level of control under § 512(c)(1)(B).[93]

Recent Legislative Activities

Some copyright holders, particularly those who create and distribute music, television programs, and movies, have publicly expressed frustration with what they consider to be an "outdated" § 512 and would like Congress to require service providers to have more responsibility in preventing infringing activity.[94] In the 113th Congress, the House Judiciary Committee, Subcommittee on Courts, Intellectual Property, and the Internet, held a hearing on March 13, 2014, specifically regarding § 512 of the Copyright Act, in which it heard testimony from witnesses about the degree to which the safe harbor is, or is not, operating well.[95] House Judiciary Committee Chairman Goodlatte expressed concern about what he referred to as a "whack-a-mole game by copyright owners" who have to deal with repeated unauthorized postings of their content.[96] He explained the issue as follows:

> By most accounts, good faith service providers have acted expeditiously in responding to Section 512 notices by removing or disabling links to infringing content.
>
> However, copyright owners are increasingly facing a scenario that simply wasn't anticipated during the enactment of 512 – the need of copyright owners to send a voluminous amount of notices seeking removal of infringing content followed by the almost immediate reappearance of the same infringing content.

At the hearing, content owners argued that § 512, as currently written and interpreted by the courts, places too much burden on copyright owners to police infringing activity online,[97] whereas service providers urged Congress to keep the current DMCA framework unchanged and instead rely upon voluntary industry agreements and private industry solutions (such as content filtering systems) to address any infringement problems.[98]

End Notes

[1] P.L. 105-304, 112 Stat. 2860 (1998) (codified at 17 U.S.C. § 512).
[2] *See* Ellison v. Robertson, 357 F.3d 1072, 1076 (9th Cir. 2004).

[3] The Digital Millennium Copyright Act of 1998: U.S. Copyright Office Summary, 8 (Dec. 1998) at http://www.copyright.gov/legislation/dmca.pdf. (Hereinafter "Copyright Office Summary.")

[4] 144 CONG. REC. S11,889 (daily ed. Oct. 2, 1998) (statement of Sen. Hatch).

[5] H.Rept. 105-796, 105th Cong., 2d Sess. 72 (1998).

[6] 17 U.S.C. § 512(a)-(d).

[7] In re Verizon Internet Servs., Inc., 240 F. Supp. 2d 24, 37 (D.D.C. 2003), *rev'd sub nom.* Recording Indus. Ass'n of Am. v. Verizon Internet Servs., Inc., 351 F.3d 1229 (D.C. Cir. 2003).

[8] Electronic Frontier Foundation, *Digital Millennium Copyright Act*, *at* http://www.eff.org /issues/dmca.

[9] 17 U.S.C. § 102(a).

[10] 17 U.S.C. § 106.

[11] "Statutory" or "compulsory" licenses compel copyright owners to allow third parties to use creative works under certain conditions and according to specific requirements, in exchange for payment of royalty fees at a rate determined by a federal government body known as the Copyright Royalty Board.

[12] 17 U.S.C. § 107.

[13] 17 U.S.C. § 501.

[14] 17 U.S.C. § 502.

[15] 17 U.S.C. § 504(b).

[16] 17 U.S.C. § 504(c)(1).

[17] 17 U.S.C. § 505.

[18] 17 U.S.C. § 302. Other terms have been established for different works and different periods of time. For a concise chart explaining the different terms, *see* http://www.copyright.cornell. edu/resources/publicdomain.cfm.

[19] Fonovisa, Inc. v. Cherry Auction, Inc., 76 F.3d 259, 264 (9th Cir. 1996).

[20] The Supreme Court in *Sony Corp. of Am. v. Universal City Studios, Inc.*, 464 U.S. 417, 435 (1984) stated: "The absence of such express language in the copyright statute does not preclude the imposition of liability for copyright infringements on certain parties who have not themselves engaged in the infringing activity. For vicarious liability is imposed in virtually all areas of the law, and the concept of contributory infringement is merely a species of the broader problem of identifying the circumstances in which it is just to hold one individual accountable for the actions of another."

[21] A & M Records, Inc. v. Napster, Inc., 239 F.3d 1004, 1019 (9th Cir. 2001).

[22] Gershwin Publ'g Corp. v. Columbia Artists Mgmt, Inc., 443 F2d. 1159, 1162 (2d. Cir. 1971).

[23] 545 U.S. 913 (2005).

[24] *Id.* at 923; *see also* Columbia Pictures Industries, Inc. v. Fung, 710 F.3d 1020, 1034 (9th Cir. 2013).

[25] Ellison v. Robertson, 189 F. Supp. 2d 1051, 1064 (C.D. Cal. 2002), *aff'd in part and rev'd in part*, 357 F.3d 1072 (9th Cir. 2004). Service providers who qualify for safe harbor are protected from all monetary and most equitable relief that may arise from copyright liability. In such a situation, "even if a plaintiff can show that a safe harbor-eligible service provider has violated her copyright, the plaintiff will only be entitled to the limited injunctive relief set forth in 17 U.S.C. § 512(j)." Corbis Corp. v. Amazon.com, Inc., 351 F. Supp. 2d 1090, 1098-99 (W.D. Wash. 2004) (citations omitted).

[26] 17 U.S.C. § 512(a)-(d).

[27] 17 U.S.C. § 512(k)(1)(A).

[28] 17 U.S.C. § 512(k)(1)(B).

[29] H.Rept. 105-551, pt. 2 at 64.

[30] 17 U.S.C. § 512(i)(1)(A)-(B).

[31] "Standard technical measures" is defined at § 512(i)(2).

[32] 17 U.S.C. § 512(n).

[33] 17 U.S.C. § 512(a).

[34] *Id.*

[35] Caching is defined as "intermediate and temporary storage of material on a system or network operated by the service provider." 17 U.S.C. § 512(b).

[36] *Copyright Office Summary,* at 10.

[37] 17 U.S.C. § 512(b)(2)(A)-(E).

[38] H.Rept. 105-551, pt. 2, 105th Cong. 2d Sess. 53 (1998).

[39] 17 U.S.C. § 512(c).

[40] 17 U.S.C. § 512(c)(1)(A)(ii).

[41] 17 U.S.C. § 512(c)(1)(A)(iii).

[42] "The Register of Copyrights is directed to maintain a directory of designated agents available for inspection by the public, both on the website of the Library of Congress, and in hard copy format on file at the Copyright Office." H.Rept. 105-551, pt. 2 at 55.

[43] 17 U.S.C. § 512(c)(3)(A)(i)-(vi).

[44] 17 U.S.C. § 512(d).

[45] 17 U.S.C. § 512(d)(1)-(3).

[46] H.Rept. 105-551, pt. 2 at 58.

[47] *See* 17 U.S.C. § 512(b)(E), (c)(C), and (d)(3).

[48] "'Knowingly' means that a party actually knew, should have known if it acted with reasonable care or diligence, or would have had no substantial doubt had it been acting in good faith, that it was making misrepresentations. 'Material' means that the misrepresentation affected the ISP's response to a DMCA letter." Online Policy Group v. Diebold, Inc., 337 F. Supp. 2d 1195, 1204 (N.D. Cal. 2004) (citations omitted).

[49] 17 U.S.C. § 512(j)(1)(A).

[50] *See* Columbia Pictures Industries, Inc. v. Fung, 710 F.3d 1020, 1039 (9th Cir. 2013).

[51] 17 U.S.C. § 512(m)(1).

[52] 488 F.3d 1102, 1113 (9th Cir. 2007).

[53] 718 F. Supp. 2d 514, 524 (S.D.N.Y. 2010).

[54] *Id.* at 526, *citing* 17 U.S.C. § 512(k)(1)(B).

[55] *Id.* at 527. *See also* UMG Recordings, Inc. v. Shelter Capital Partners LLC, 718 F.3d 1006, 1016 (9th Cir. 2013) (finding that the § 512(c) safe harbor extends to infringement resulting not just from the provider's storage of UGC, but also any services that the provider operates to facilitate users' access to the material).

[56] 357 F.3d 1072 (9th Cir. 2004)

[57] *Id.* at 1080.

[58] *Id.*

[59] *Id.*

[60] 239 F.3d 619, 620 (4th Cir. 2001).

[61] *Id.* at 624.

[62] *Id.* at 624-25. The court further explained, "[W]hen a letter provides notice equivalent to a list of representative works that can be easily identified by the service provider, the notice substantially complies with the notification requirements." *Id.* at 625.

[63] *Id.* at 620 (emphasis in original).

[64] 17 U.S.C. § 512(c)(1)(A)(i), (iii).

[65] Viacom Int'l, Inc. v. YouTube, Inc., 718 F. Supp. 2d 514, 523-24 (S.D.N.Y. 2010) ("To let knowledge of a generalized practice of infringement in the industry, or of a proclivity of users to post infringing materials, impose responsibility on service providers to discover which of their users' postings infringe a copyright would contravene the structure and operation of the DMCA.").

[66] *Id.* at 523. *See also* Viacom Int'l, Inc. v. YouTube, Inc., 676 F.3d 19, 26 (2d Cir. 2012) (hold that "the District Court correctly held that the § 512(c) safe harbor requires knowledge or awareness of specific infringing activity.").

[67] *Id.* at 30.

[68] 351 F. Supp. 2d 1090 (W.D. Wash. 2004).

[69] "The zShops platform allows individuals and retailers (referred to as 'vendors') to showcase their products and sell them directly to online consumers. Amazon, however, does not sell any of its own inventory on the zShops platform." Id. at 1094.

[70] *Id.* at 1096-97.

[71] *Id.* at 1107.

[72] UMG Recordings, Inc. v. Shelter Capital Partners LLC, 718 F.3d 1006 (9th Cir. 2013).

[73] *Id.* at 1020, *citing Corbis Corp. v. Amazon.com, Inc.*, 351 F. Supp. 2d 1090 (W.D. Wash. 2004).

[74] *Id.* at 1021.

[75] *Id.* at 1022.

[76] 17 U.S.C. § 512(c)(1)(A)(ii), (iii).

[77] 488 F.3 1102, 1114 (9th Cir. 2007).

[78] *Id.*

[79] Viacom Int'l, Inc. v. YouTube, Inc., 676 F.3d 19, 31 (2d Cir. 2012).

[80] Global-Tech Appliances, Inc. v. SEB S.A., 131 S. Ct. 2060, 2068-69 (2011).

[81] *Id.* at 2069 (emphasis added).

[82] For more information on this decision, *see* CRS Report R41976, *Intent Standard for Induced Patent Infringement: Global-Tech Appliances, Inc. v. SEB S.A.* , by Brian T. Yeh.

[83] *Global-Tech,* 131 S. Ct. at 2070 (citing various opinions of the Courts of Appeals that have articulated the doctrine).

[84] *Id.*

[85] *Id.* at 2070-71. (citations omitted).

[86] Viacom Int'l, Inc. v. YouTube, Inc., 676 F.3d 19, 35 (2d Cir. 2012).

[87] 718 F.3d 1006, 1023 (9th Cir. 2013).

[88] *Id.*

[89] 17 U.S.C. § 512(c)(1)(B).

[90] *Viacom*, 676 F.3d at 38.

[91] *Id.*

[92] 213 F. Supp. 2d 1146, 1173 (C.D. Cal. 2002).

[93] *Viacom*, 676 F.3d at 38.

[94] Nathan Pollard, *Panelists Debate Intentions of DMCA and Who Is Liable Under YouTube Decision,* BNA'S PATENT, TRADEMARK & COPYRIGHT JOURNAL, Aug. 5, 2011; Bill Donahue, *Google, Others Clash Over DMCA Safe Harbor,* Law360.com, Mar. 13, 2014.

[95] *Section 512 of Title 17: Hearing Before the House Judiciary Committee, Subcommittee on Courts, Intellectual Property, and the Internet,* 113th Cong., 2d Sess. (2014).

[96] *Id.* (opening remarks by Chairman Goodlatte).

[97] *Id.* (statement of Professor Sean M. O'Connor).
[98] *Id.* (statement of Katherine Oyama, Senior Copyright Policy Counsel, Google).

INDEX

C

G

H

I

J

K

L

M

N

O

P

R

S

T

U

V

W

Y